Herr Lubitsch Goes to Hollywood

Herr Lubitsch Goes to Hollywood

German and American Film after World War I

Kristin Thompson

Amsterdam University Press

Cover photograph: Ernst Lubitsch at work on his first Hollywood film, Rosita (courtesy the Academy of Motion Picture Arts and Sciences)

Cover design: Kok Korpershoek, Amsterdam
Lay-out: JAPES, Amsterdam

ISBN 90 5356 709 7 (hardcover)
ISBN 90 5356 708 9 (paperback)
NUR 674

© Amsterdam University Press, Amsterdam, 2005

For Paolo

Contents

Acknowledgements

This book traces its existence back to a wonderful conference hosted at the University of East Anglia in December of 1983 and organized by Thomas Elsaesser: "Space, Frame, Narrative: Ernst Lubitsch, Silent Cinema 1916-26." I am grateful to Thomas and the staff of that conference for having planted the seed that led, much later, to this book. The paper that I presented at their conference sat in a file folder for many years, during which I have pursued other projects that involved watching German films, including those by Lubitsch and also about 75 "ordinary" German films (i.e., not German Expressionist, not *Kammerspiel*, not *Neue Sachlichkeit*). My main focus of study was German Expressionism, to which movement Lubitsch did not belong. He seemed, however, too important – and attractive – a figure to ignore. His films have so far been accorded far less close study than they deserve. Eventually, it also became apparent that Lubitsch could provide a way to compare normative styles in American and German films of the last decade of the silent era, for here was a filmmaker who, uniquely, was a master of both national styles and the director most highly respected by his colleagues in both countries. My gratitude to Thomas continues, for this examination of Lubitsch has come full circle and returned to his diligent care in the final publication. My thanks to him and to the University of Amsterdam Press for making it possible to present this analytical study with the numerous illustrations that it required.

I am grateful for the vital assistance I received during my research from various people and institutions: Kitte Vinke and the staff of the Deutsches Filminstitut-DIF, Frankfurt am Main; Klaus Volkmer of the Münchener Filmmuseum; Gabrielle Claes and the staff of the Cinémathèque Royale de Belgique; Paolo Cherchi Usai, Caroline Yeager, and the staff of the Motion Picture Department of the International Museum of Photography at the George Eastman House; Matti Lukkarila, Timo Matoniemi, and the staff of the Suomen Elokuva-Arkisto, Helsinki; the staff of the Margaret Herrick Library of the Academy of Motion Picture Arts and Sciences; and the devoted organizers of La Giornate del Cinema Muto, Pordenone and Sacile, Italy.

Considerable thanks are due to Peter von Bagh and Michael Campi for providing invaluable research materials. Ben Brewster, Lea Jacobs, and the faculty and students of the weekly Colloquium meeting of the Dept. of Communication Arts at the University of Wisconsin-Madison, have over the years offered helpful comments on presentations of early versions of these chapters. Jake Black has been of immense assistance in preparing the many illustrations. David Bordwell has shared with me a love of Lubitsch, as he has shared so many other things, for decades. His comments and suggestions have greatly improved this book.

Introduction

Lubitsch: The Filmmakers' Filmmaker

In film-studies circles, Ernst Lubitsch is recognized as one of the great directors of world cinema, but the general public has long ceased to know his name. Even mentioning NINOTCHKA usually brings no responsive smile of recognition.

Filmmakers, however, still love Lubitsch. They apparently recognize in him not just one of the medium's premiere storytellers but a consummate master of every technical aspect of the cinema. Shortly after Lubitsch's death, Jeannette MacDonald said of him:

> On the set, he had the greatness of his art, but no "artiness." I have known so many directors who idealized him and styled some part of his work in their own careers. And to me, he was the greatest cutter in the business. Only Thanksgiving night he was talking of the lack of knowledge of cutting among some current directors. He cut as he worked on the set – that is, he shot just what he wanted. He visualized in the script the precise way he wanted it to work on the screen and I never knew him to be in trouble on a picture. He whipped his troubles in script. His scripts were almost invariably his pictures.[1]

This sense of precision and mastery of the art of film recalls another great American master of the comic form, Buster Keaton.

The admiration has continued ever since. In the introduction to Peter Bogdanovich's collection of interviews he conducted over many years with most of the great Hollywood directors, he devoted a section to "The Director I Never Met" and wrote, "Lubitsch is also the one director whom nearly every other director I ever interviewed mentioned with respect and awe as among the very best."[2] Billy Wilder was fond of mentioning a sign he used for guidance: "For many years, I had that sign on my wall. HOW WOULD LUBITSCH DO IT? I would *always* look at it when I was writing a script or planning a picture. 'What kind of track would Lubitsch be on? How would he make this look natural?' Lubitsch was my influence as a director."[3] In 1998, *Newsweek's* special issue on movies included a claim by director Cameron Crowe that Lubitsch was still the model for makers of comedies.[4] During recent correspondence with producer Barrie M. Osborne about my research on THE LORD OF THE RINGS I mentioned that I was finishing up a book on Lubitsch, to which he immediately replied that he would like to have a copy.

Thus it is hardly necessary to argue the point in claiming that Lubitsch was a master of two national styles. He was recognized as such among professionals then. He is recognized as such among professionals now. The question is, then, what can this master tell us about the mutual influence of two great national cinemas?

Lubitsch's Place in Two National Cinemas

This book is only in part about Lubitsch. The interested reader will, I hope, learn a good deal about the director's work in the silent era, but the subject matter here is more ambitious. I intend to specify the major differences between the norms of stylistic practice in the two most powerful producing countries at the end of World War I: the United States and Germany. In my chapters of *The Classical Hollywood Cinema*, I analyzed how the guidelines of continuity-style storytelling emerged and coalesced during the 1910s. No one has attempted a comparable analysis of the assumptions and ordinary practice of filmmakers in Germany during that period, and this book attempts to fill that gap. Beyond that, I shall also examine the influences that these two countries' cinemas had on each other, and how the differences between their stylistic norms diminished noticeably in the decade after the war.

Lubitsch never sought to create highly artistic or avant-garde works in the manner of his famous contemporaries, F. W. Murnau and Fritz Lang. Instead he aimed to craft his films with broad appeal using the most up-to-date techniques. Thus this great master of two national film styles provides a neat and straightforward way to study those styles in this period of great change, as the "golden ages" of both countries' cinemas were beginning.

Lubitsch's career provides an almost unique example of a filmmaker working during the studio era who was at the top of one national cinema, moved to another, and became its leading director as well. The most obvious comparison would be to Hitchcock, but he had the advantage of establishing himself in the British film industry of the 1920s and 1930s, an industry which essentially modeled its own filmmaking practice on Hollywood guidelines. For Hitchcock, the move did not involve adopting a different approach to filmmaking – only carrying on the same basic style with much larger budgets. Moreover, Hitchcock did not achieve a summit of prominence as rapidly; rather, his high reputation today stems mainly from critical re-evaluation relatively late in his career. In contrast, Lubitsch came from a country where a distinctly different set of norms of filmmaking were in place. Upon his arrival in Hollywood, he was also hailed as *the* master – a position he essentially inherited because D. W.

Griffith's career was on the decline. In this book I shall focus on Lubitsch's work in the postwar era, his films from the years 1918 to 1927.

Lubitsch was born in Berlin and began his film career in 1913 by starring in and eventually directing a series of successful comic shorts. He rose to wider prominence in 1918 when he began directing costume pictures (e.g., CARMEN, 1918, MADAME DUBARRY, 1919) and satirical comedies (DIE AUSTERINPRINZESSIN, 1919). Lubitsch gained international fame when MADAME DUBARRY broke barriers of post-war anti-German sentiment and became an international hit. He was soon the most famous German director at home and abroad, and, not surprisingly, he was lured to Hollywood in 1922. Less predictably, he easily mastered the recently formulated classical style that had come into use during the war years. While his fellow émigrés like E. A. Dupont and F. W. Murnau had short-lived and disappointing stays in Hollywood, Lubitsch's American career proved productive and long-lasting. He died in 1947, having made roughly half of THAT LADY IN ERMINE for 20th Century-Fox. (The film was completed by Otto Preminger.)

Lubitsch's growing success came in a period which saw widespread and long-lasting changes in the cinema – perhaps more than in any other era. Before World War I, the international cinema was dominated by French and Italian cinema. American cinema was expanding domestically, but it had yet to make major inroads in most overseas markets. During the war, however, production declined in France and Italy, and the American firms quickly stepped in to supply films to theaters in many territories. Once hostilities ended, Hollywood films were firmly entrenched, and other countries found themselves struggling to keep a substantial share of their domestic markets, let alone compete with America internationally.[5]

The war had, ironically, strengthened the German industry. In 1916, the government banned the import of all but Danish films. This ban was kept in place until December 31, 1920. Thus, for nearly five years, German film production was free to expand, and the industry emerged from the war second in size and strength only to Hollywood. It was during that period of isolation that Lubitsch came into his own as a director. He became the finest proponent of the German approach to filmmaking, a style which was largely the same as the one used in most European producing countries.

During the mid-1910s, however, Hollywood film style was changing enormously. What has been termed the "classical" style emerged, the underlying principle of which was to tailor film technique perfectly to tell a story as comprehensibly and unobtrusively as possible. Scenes were broken up into closer shots through analytical editing, shifting the spectator's eye to the most salient part of the action at each moment. Filming interior scenes in diffused light in the open air or in glass-sided studios was largely abandoned in favor of "dark" studios illuminated entirely by artificial lighting. This multi-directional lighting, designed to pick characters out against muted backgrounds and to model their bodies more three-dimensionally, became codified as "three-point" lighting. Acting styles became less broad, depending more on glances and small gestures than on pantomime. Set design evolved to make the space containing the action simpler and hence less distracting.

Once Hollywood films began screening in Germany in 1921, German filmmakers noticed and absorbed the new stylistic traits, and Lubitsch was in the forefront of this change. His German films of 1921 and 1922 reflect his new knowledge of classical technique, and he was clearly ready to make the leap into Hollywood filmmaking even before he went there. Once in America, he rapidly honed his application of classical principles, and soon he was in turn influencing the filmmakers there with a string of masterpieces, including THE MARRIAGE CIRCLE (1924) and LADY WINDERMERE'S FAN (1925).

The postwar years in Europe could have become quite competitive, because producers in countries like Italy, England, France, and Germany were not at all sure that Hollywood would continue to dominate world markets. Producers hoped that the balance would shift back to those European countries that had managed to improve their production values and make films with international appeal. Style was a big issue in creating such appeal, and the German press discussed techniques like three-point lighting.

One result was that classical Hollywood practice exerted a considerable influence on German films of the 1920s, from 1921 on. Despite the fact that the German classics we see today are mostly Expressionist or part of the *Neue Sachlichkeit* tendency, ordinary German films – and hundreds of these were made each year in this prolific industry – looked more and more like their Hollywood counterparts. Later in the decade, to be sure, distinctively German techniques like the *entfesselte Kamera* (the unchained or freely moving camera), montage sequences, and false-perspective sets made their way to Hollywood. Nevertheless, the strongest flow of influence was from Hollywood to Germany.

The Standard Story: Germany Escapes Hollywood's Influence

In writing a revisionist account of the German silent cinema, I would ideally at this point like to skewer an old myth perpetuated in traditional historians' writings. I would cite claims by Georges Sadoul, Jean Mitry, Paul Rotha, Lewis Jacobs, or Arthur Knight to the effect that Hollywood had no influence on German cinema in the post-World War I years. There is, alas, no such myth, because the notion that Hollywood could have influenced German cinema in that period seems never to have occurred to any historian. Rather, the standard story has Hollywood influence creeping into Germany in the second half of the 1920s, just as American producers were stealing away the country's great filmmakers. Thus the decline of Germany's golden age of cinema could be blamed largely on its larger, less artistic transatlantic rival – and for this particular myth, there are plenty of historians to cite.

Historians tend to group German films of the 1920s into broad trends: historical epics, Expressionist films, *Kammerspiel* films, and/or a tendency variously described as street films, *Neue Sachlichkeit* ("New Objectivity"), or simply realism. Germany emerges as the home of artistic cinema, untainted by Hollywood's more commercially oriented, popular style. Historians typically point out in passing that Germany was turning out hundreds of films a year that did not fall into these trends but instead were mainstream genre pictures. Lubitsch, who produced some of the most financially successful films of the years immediately after the war, functions as the chief – and usually only – representative of this more commercial cinema. How Lubitsch relates to that mainstream cinema is not discussed.

Based only on the most prominent and usually most artistic films of the era, historians could easily conclude that the German cinema was so distinctive that it was somehow impervious to influences from Hollywood for a remarkably long time after the war. For example, Paul Rotha's influential *The Film Till Now* (often updated but originally published in 1930), recognized that Hollywood strongly influenced German filmmaking in the 1920s – but only later in the decade. Primarily interested in artistic film styles, Rotha recalled that in the mid-1920s, "It was general to look to the German cinema for the real uses of the film medium ... It became customary to believe that a film coming from a German studio, made by a German director, cameraman, architect, and actors would be of a certain interest." After the mid-1920s, according to Rotha,

> The real German film died quietly. Many of its creators went to Hollywood, while those who remained joined with fresh commercialized minds in the complete reorganization of their industry on American principles. Hollywood took interest in her rival, nourished her, but stole her talent. The German cinema became American in its outlook and its characteristics became imitative of Hollywood.[6]

For traditional historians, influence becomes important only with DER LETZTE MANN in 1924, and the influence flows from Germany into other countries, mainly the US. That influence has been greatly exaggerated, since historians usually link the release of THE LAST LAUGH in the US with the subsequent immigration of a few of the most prominent German auteurs to the American studios. Arthur Knight's influential 1957 world survey, THE LIVELIEST ART, claimed that Murnau's film "hastened the already apparent Germanization of Hollywood's studios," adding that German personnel, themes, acting, and "above all, production techniques" dominated American filmmaking into the sound era.[7]

Knight considerably exaggerates the extent of Germany's influence on American filmmaking. Although Murnau, Dimitri Buchowetsky, and Paul Leni were much-touted imports to America, along with several prominent German actors, scenarists, and cinematographers, they made up only a tiny portion of the total number of filmmakers in Hollywood. Moreover, both Buchowetsky and Murnau proved disappointments to their new employers, and Leni's death in 1929 robbed the American studios of their second most successful German director, after Lubitsch. The vast majority of German filmmakers stayed put, however, continuing to make hundreds of films a year – most of them imitating the classical Hollywood style. German Expressionism undoubtedly influenced the brooding style of the nascent horror-film genre that developed at Universal in the late 1920s (most notably with Leni's THE CAT AND THE CANARY, 1927), and later the film-noir movies of the 1940s, but it had little impact on other genres.

The implication of the standard story, then, is that Germany managed to create a distinctive national cinema, free from the influences of Hollywood. That cinema consisted of Expressionist films, the occasional *Kammerspiel*, and later, *Neue Sachlichkeit*. The fact that some of the world's great directors – Murnau, Lang, G. W. Pabst – and some important lesser lights – Leni, Dupont, Robert Wiene, Paul Czinner – worked in these areas makes it all the easier to construct a national cinema that seems to consist largely of untainted art films. Yet, as we have seen, the vast majority of German films fell into none of these categories, instead drawing upon rudimentary continuity editing and the more old-fashioned diffused lighting. Lubitsch's work was simply the best among these popularly oriented films, but he rapidly absorbed the new style of Hollywood once he became exposed to it. More slowly, so did his colleagues in the German film industry.

1 Lubitsch's Career

Studying the Conditions of Influence

The Russian Formalist literary theorist Jurij Tynjanov has pointed out that the historian who searches for influence treads a difficult path. The devices an artist borrows from other works may be so transformed in his or her hands as to be unrecognizable to the observer. Here the artist's own declaration of having been influenced is the crucial evidence needed for the historian to realize that influence has probably taken place (unless the artist is lying or self-deceiving). Tynjanov mentions another danger, in which the same device is used in different artworks at the same time – and yet this apparent case of influence is in fact merely a coincidence. Two or more artists have introduced similar devices independently. During World War I, directors in different countries employed cuts involving graphic matches; these filmmakers most likely did not see each other's work, but they hit upon similar ways of exploring film style.

Tynjanov sums up the subject of literary influence succinctly: "Influence can occur at such a time and in such a direction as literary conditions permit."[1] The same is true in film. When we speak of studying influences, we are necessarily studying mental events, which are never completely recoverable. But when we study artists' mental events, we are dealing with people who have left considerable traces of influences, in their artworks and often in their words, in interviews and writings. Moreover, filmmakers depend to a large extent on companies and on collaboration with their casts and crews. The coordination of all these people and their contributions to a film often involves a set of shared principles and guidelines, sometimes expressed explicitly in "how-to" texts, sometimes implicit in the stylistic similarities among artworks. In some cases, the films and the texts relating to them, along with a knowledge of the overall filmmaking context of the day, allow us to make rather precise statements and arguments about the conditions of influence. Ernst Lubitsch and the post-World War I German cinema provide a particularly clear case of profound and sudden influences from a single source – Hollywood cinema – upon a great filmmaker and the national cinema of which he was the most illustrious member.

Lubitsch himself declared that he was strongly influenced by Hollywood films, but by examining the conditions of influence, we can specify how and when the changes took place. We can help define the differences between Lubitsch's early features and his later ones. Lubitsch's early career took place in circumstances unique in film history, where a ban on imports left German filmmakers isolated from outside influences for nearly five years. After the ban was lifted, the sudden influx of foreign films, particularly from Hollywood, had an immediate impact on German filmmaking. Under such circumstances, influences occurred with dramatic speed; they become more apparent than in more ordinary situations.

During the period before World War I, films circulated freely among countries. Something of an international style developed. Individual filmmakers or firms in a single country might create distinctive innovations, but these were quickly copied in other countries. World War I altered the situation, cutting off some countries from foreign markets and foreign influence. In rare cases, a country's filmmaking might exist in near isolation, creating the possibility for a distinctive national cinema to arise. This happened most notably in Sweden, Russia, and, somewhat later, Germany.

During the spring of 1916, the German government barred the importation of certain expendable goods, including motion pictures. The official purpose of the ban was to improve Germany's balance of trade and to bolster its currency. The flow of imports was cut to a trickle. After the war's end, this ban remained in effect until it finally expired at midnight on December 31, 1920. Thanks to a government quota and a weak currency, foreign films appeared only gradually on the German market. In 1921, German cinema emerged from years of artificially created isolation.

The start of the ban happened to coincide closely with the period in 1916 when American film exports burgeoned and its industry began to dominate world film markets. After 1916, this American expansion hurt the countries which had formerly been the top two sources of films: France and Italy. After the war, neither country was able to counter American competition and regain its former status. In Germany, however, the situation was very different. Before the war, German films were a minor factor on the world market, and domestic exhibition was dominated by imports from America, France, and Italy. The 1916 ban boosted domestic film production, with firms multiplying and expanding. Ironically, the Germany film industry emerged in late 1918 as the second largest in the world.

Because of the ban on imports, German filmmakers had missed the crucial period when Hollywood's film style was changing rapidly and becoming standard practice. A unified, linear, easily intelligible narrative pattern was emerging in American films, and it has in its general traits remained virtually the same ever since. The continuity editing system, with its efficient methods of laying out a clear space for the action, had already been formulated by 1917. The three-point system of lighting was also taking shape. In contrast, German film style had developed relatively little during this era. Lubitsch made most of his German features while the import ban was still in place and in the two years immediately after it was lifted. As a result, he adhered to the normative German style of his day and became its most skilled practitioner. Among its norms were diffuse, unidirectional lighting and editing that did not include continuity guidelines like consistent screen direction. Once Lubitsch was exposed to classical filmmaking, he consciously adopted its influences and within a remarkably short time became one of the very best practitioners of Hollywood's style.

Lubitsch and the German Film Industry

Ernst Lubitsch was born on January 29, 1892 into a middle-class family of assimilated Jews living in Berlin. His father Simon owned a tailor shop specializing in ladies' coats, and Ernst was expected to enter the family business. He claimed he wanted to become an actor from age six, and he launched into his career at a young age and was remarkably energetic and reasonably successful in pursuing it. Beginning in 1910, at age 18, he took acting lessons from Victor Arnold, an actor with Max Reinhardt's Deutsche Theater. In the evenings he performed in slapstick acts in various vaudeville houses and cabarets. Arnold was impressed enough by the young Lubitsch that in 1911 he got his pupil a job with Reinhardt's ensemble. Lubitsch played regularly in Reinhardt productions until May of 1918. He usually had very small roles (such as the second gravedigger in HAMLET). By the time Lubitsch left the Reinhardt ensemble, as Hans Helmut Prinzler has concluded, "He had not played a real lead role there."[2]

In 1913, Lubitsch began to supplement his income by appearing in films. His first was apparently DIE IDEALE GATTIN (or EINE IDEALE GATTIN), a two-reeler about which little is known. Lubitsch's second film, however, was a considerable success: DIE FIRMA HEIRATET (1914), a comic four-reeler directed by Carl Wilhelm. Lubitsch played the lead role, Moritz Abramowsky, which popularized him as a comic actor, and the films in which he subsequently starred often cast him as a brash young Jew struggling his way to success by dubious means. He directed himself for the first time in AUF EIS GEFÜHRT, a lost 1915 film. He continued to act in his own and other directors' films. The few that survive from the war suggest that the young director adopted a simple, old-fashioned style common in comedies of the era. The films concentrate on displaying the antics of the lead character, who often turns and mugs for the camera. By common consent, Lubitsch was primarily concerned with these films as vehicles for his own performances, and it was not until his features, starting in 1918, that he began to use more complex techniques and develop a style of his own.

One can see Lubitsch's silent filmmaking as falling into four periods. First would be the stretch from 1913 to 1917, when he was primarily making comedies and acting in most of his films. The second period runs from 1918 to the first part of 1921, when he turned to higher-budget features, alternating between sophisticated comedies and costume dramas. He had a short transitional phase during 1921 and 1922, when he made two films for an American production company in Berlin; in these two films he began distinctly to display the influences of Hollywood films. Finally, from 1923 to 1927, he made his silent American films. This book focuses on the second, third, and fourth periods: from 1918 to 1927.

Throughout this decade, Lubitsch was fortunate enough to work for a series of reasonably large production companies, both in Berlin and Hollywood. Early on he gathered around him a core team of personnel, some of whom stayed with him for several films, and a few of whom even followed him when he went to the US. This consistency of collaborators may help explain how Lubitsch was able to turn out so many films (the shortest being three-reelers) with such consistently high quality in the immediate post-war years: nineteen films in the five years from 1918 to 1922! Hanns Kräly wrote or co-wrote most of Lubitsch's films (the most notable exceptions were THE MARRIAGE CIRCLE and LADY WINDERMERE'S FAN) from 1915 to Lubitsch's last silent feature, ETERNAL LOVE, in 1929. Cinematographer Theodor Sparkuhl, originally a newsreel cameraman, worked occasionally for Lubitsch starting in 1916, and he shot all of the director's features from 1918 to 1922. Kurt Richter designed the sets for many of the director's films. Ali Hubert created costumes for him in both Germany and the US. Lubitsch's acting ensemble included regulars Harry Liedtke, Victor Jansson, Margarete Kupfer, Emil Jannings, Ossi Oswalda, Pola Negri, and, less frequently, Henny Porten.

Considering his rather modest beginnings as a performer in short comedies, Lubitsch was able to rise spectacularly within German filmmaking circles, going from short farces to historical epics like MADAME DUBARRY very quickly, within a two-year period (1918-1919). He was able to do this in part because he happened to be working primarily for a company that became part of Germany's most powerful film conglomerate. That company was Union, which originated as a theater chain established by Paul Davidson in 1905. As the chain expanded, it acquired the name Projektions 'Union' A.G. in 1910 and branched out into distribution. Finally, in 1912, Davidson moved Union into production as well. In 1913, he constructed a studio facility at Berlin-Tempelhof. Coincidentally, that same year another firm, Deutsche Bioscop, built its studio at Babelsberg, a Berlin suburb. Although Lubitsch made a few

films for other companies early in his career, his two big early successes, DIE
FIRMA HEIRATET and DER STOLZ DER FIRMA, were Union productions, and by
1915 he was working exclusively for Davidson. Over the next two years, he
made many two- and three-reelers, most of which are now lost.[3]

A turning point in Lubitsch's career, and in the German industry in general,
came in December, 1918. At that point, several small firms, including Union
and Deutsch Bioscop, were combined under one umbrella group, the Universum-Film Aktiengesellschaft, or UFA. That group was ten times as large as any
earlier German film company. Davidson became one of UFA's board of directors and had a considerable hand in assigning personnel and determining
budgets. Still, the various production companies within UFA continued to
function with a considerable degree of independence. While UFA consolidated distribution and exhibition, its individual producers continued to compete with each other. They tended to specialize in different genres, with Union
concentrating on costume films and frivolous comedies.[4]

Jan-Christopher Horak has argued that from SCHUHPALAST PINKUS (1916)
on, Lubitsch's films move from slapstick to satire and take on a technical sophistication in their sets and lighting that was not typical of comparable productions of the period. By 1917, he claims, Lubitsch's comedies were so successful that Davidson allotted them bigger budgets. Indeed, large budgets
were one way by which UFA hoped to make films that could compete with
Hollywood on the world market. In 1918, Davidson suggested that Lubitsch
try making one of the "Grossfilme," or large films – four of which were produced at UFA that year. Lubitsch hesitated, but the move would allow him
greater possibilities in the way of sets and costumes. He agreed to make an exotic thriller, DIE AUGEN DER MUMIE MÂ. Davidson wanted him to use Pola
Negri, and Lubitsch also cast his regulars, Harry Liedtke and Emil Jannings.
The film was a hit and sent Lubitsch off in a new direction. Lubitsch used
Negri and Liedtke again in CARMEN and created another hit. Indeed, Horak
has suggested that these two films were what allowed UFA to make a profit –
barely, at one percent – that year.[5]

Davidson and Lubitsch followed this banner year with another, giving UFA
three more hits in 1919: DIE AUSTERNPRINZESSIN, MADAME DUBARRY, and DIE
PUPPE. MADAME DUBARRY was not only a critical success, but it was also the
first film to be shown in a number of key foreign markets, most notably in the
US. Quite apart from its high revenues, Lubitsch's film was seen as a major
strategic achievement for the film industry as a whole, since there was strong
anti-German sentiment in many countries. All this success meant that
Lubitsch could essentially do anything he wanted to – and he chose to start off
1920 with two broad rustic comedies in a row, both pastiches of Shakespeare
plays: KOHLHIESELS TÖCHTER (THE TAMING OF THE SHREW) and ROMEO UND

Julia im Schnee.[6] This pair of films is often dismissed as assigned projects that he considered beneath him – but given his considerable freedom at that point in his career, they were clearly his own preference.[7] They were very popular then and are still amusing today. Indeed, the only Lubitsch film of this era that seems to have failed at the box office was DIE BERGKATZE – a fact that may strike modern viewers as odd, since it seems like just another sophisticated, stylized comedy, resembling DIE AUSTERNPRINZESSIN and DIE PUPPE. Perhaps it went just a bit too far in its comic Expressionist settings, but at any rate, Lubitsch never tried anything of the sort again. Some idea of Lubitsch's worth to UFA can be gathered from a contemporary estimate that ANNA BOLEYN cost about eight million Marks to produce, and its sale in the US would fetch $200,000, or the equivalent of fourteen million Marks.[8]

All of Lubitsch's films for Davidson were made at the large Union studio in Tempelhof, an open district of Berlin that now contains the city's second airport. Davidson had built the studio in 1913. Like other European studios of the era, its walls were glass, to allow for filming in sunlight, and it was furnished with frames for hanging supplemental electric lamps above the sets. The filming space was 20 by 40 meters, or 800 square meters. The studio occupied about 90,000 square meters.[9] Thus Lubitsch had plenty of space for the large outdoor settings of his epic productions. The studio could also accommodate interior sets of a considerable size, though huge sets like the interior of Westminster Cathedral in ANNA BOLEYN were built in the open air and lit by direct sunlight. This kind of studio facility allowed for the reuse of standing exterior sets and encouraged filming under diffuse light coming from a single direction.

After directing a remarkable seventeen films from 1918 to 1921 in this studio, Lubitsch left Union and UFA. I have suggested that Lubitsch had the luxury of a running start into his Hollywood career in the form of a contract with an American-owned company producing in Berlin. This was the Europäische Film-Allianz, officially founded in April of 1921 as an American-German company. Ultimately the EFA stemmed from an ill-fated attempt on the part of Famous Players-Lasky [FP-L] and its distribution wing Paramount to produce films abroad. Their initial, and only, attempts along these lines occurred in the United Kingdom, Germany, and India. The immediate founder of EFA was the Hamilton Theatrical Corp., which was half-owned by FP-L; UFA also had holdings in EFA. EFA either invested in smaller production companies or contracted the distribution rights for their films. These initially included Joe-May-Film GmbH, Ernst-Lubitsch-Film GmbH (founded in December, 1920), and companies headed by Henny Porten and Ossi Oswalda. Hamilton Theatrical already had links to Lubitsch, having purchased the American rights for MADAME DUBARRY. Davidson had already decided not to renew his contract with

UFA in December, 1920, when the negotiations for the founding of EFA were presumably already underway. The rising inflation which would eventually spiral into hyperinflation was limiting Davidson's financial freedom within UFA, and some of his lead actors were receiving feelers from American production companies. Davidson wanted to form a company for Lubitsch, and the EFA provided that opportunity. Lubitsch was able to bring some of his key collaborators with him, including scriptwriter Kräly, cinematographer Sparkuhl, and designer Richter.[10] Lubitsch also realized that working for a company perceived as at least partly American would help more German films break into the American market: "The connection with America had extraordinary business advantages. The films can be advertised completely differently over there. Also, it seems to be the land of the greatest profit for the German film industry."[11]

The EFA set out to create the most modern studio in Europe, outfitted with state-of-the-art American equipment, including lamps and cameras. In 1920, a large exhibition hall in the Zoo area of Berlin had been converted to a film production studio. Unlike earlier film studios, its walls were not of glass. When converted, it became the country's largest production facility, as well as Germany's first "dark" studio, a type that had become increasingly common in America since 1915. Such studios were designed to be lit entirely artificially, allowing the filmmakers more control over the look of the shots. The EFA took over the Zoo studio in April of 1921. It was nearly three times the size of Union's main studio building, being 30 by 75 meters, or 2250 square meters, and it was equipped with all the major types of American lighting equipment.[12]

An American observer visiting the EFA studio in 1922 to observe Lubitsch at work on DIE FLAMME remarked on the facility: "When I entered the Lubitsch studio I felt as though I had been plunged suddenly from Berlin into the depths of Hollywood. There were the same treacherous cables to ensnare your brogues, the same, or almost the same, arc lights, spots and banks."[13] And indeed Lubitsch had seized upon the opportunity to use American equipment. His first film for the EFA was a spectacle at least on a par with his earlier historical epics: DAS WEIB DES PHARAO. Production photographs taken during the shooting show multiple cameras in use (Fig. 1.1). These include mostly old-style wooden cameras, including some Pathés, the most commonly used camera in Europe. But there are also three of the up-to-date metal Bell & Howells, the standard camera in Hollywood during the 1910s. Not surprisingly, the two films Lubitsch made for the EFA display a strong American stylistic influence. He was well along the way toward making a new career, one that would see him hailed as the master of Hollywood filmmaking.

The next step along that way was a brief trip to the US that Lubitsch made with Paul Davidson in late 1921. Arriving in New York on December 24, they explained to the *Moving Picture World* that they wanted to study American production methods: "Both are coming to America under the auspices of the Hamilton Theatrical Corporation to spend a month in studying American methods of film production."[14] A short time later the same journal gave some details of Lubitsch's plans: "He will stay about ten more days in New York and vicinity and then visit Los Angeles. His visit in this country will consume about six weeks. In that time he expects to gather a wealth of detail about American production methods."[15] In the end, Lubitsch actually only stayed for about a month, returning to Germany on January 17, 1922, without visiting Los Angeles. Robert Florey, writing about two years later, gave a different reason for Lubitsch's visit:

> For a long time the management of "Famous Players Lasky Paramount" [sic] sought to hire Ernst Lubitsch, and the latter had already come, two years ago, to New York, in the hope of negotiating with this company. Since his contract with E.F.A. had not ended, however, he was obliged to return to Germany, where in due course he completed his work.[16]

This account squares a bit better with Lubitsch's relatively short stay. He ended up not working at Paramount until he made FORBIDDEN PARADISE, his fourth Hollywood film, for that company in 1924.

Upon his return to Germany, Lubitsch fulfilled his EFA contract by making DIE FLAMME. Mary Pickford offered him a contract to direct her in a film. Initially she sent Lubitsch a German translation of the script for a project called DOROTHY VERNON OF HADDON HALL, but upon reading he suggested that they film FAUST instead. Biographer Scott Eyman says an anti-German backlash caused this idea to be dropped. Lubitsch's costume designer Ali Hubert wrote in 1929 that Pickford's company decided that the American public would not accept her as an unwed mother in a film with an unhappy ending. For whatever reason, the project was dropped. Lubitsch arrived in Hollywood in December of 1922, and in January Lubitsch showed Pickford the script of ROSITA.[17] (DOROTHY VERNON, 1924, became Pickford's next project after ROSITA, directed by Marshall Neilan.)

Late in her life, Pickford maintained that she and Lubitsch had not seen eye to eye and that ROSITA was a bad film and a commercial failure.[18] Yet contemporary evidence amply disproves Pickford's later claims. Drawing upon documents from the legal files of United Artists, Scott Eyman demonstrates that Pickford in fact was pleased with ROSITA and hoped to keep Lubitsch on as her director for future projects, but that the financing was not available.[19] A closer examination of these documents further clarifies the situation, including why United Artists could not afford to keep Lubitsch on after ROSITA.

Certainly few reviewers thought that ROSITA was bad. On the contrary, most lauded the film and singled Pickford out for praise. Pickford's correspondence with Dennis F. O'Brien (Pickford and Douglas Fairbanks' counsel and a vice president of United Artists from its founding) indicates that she admired Lubitsch. On June 18, 1923, a few weeks after the shooting phase of ROSITA was completed, Pickford wrote to O'Brien "I am very pleased with ROSITA and think it will be well received." A few days earlier, on June 13, Pickford had written a letter concerning Lubitsch to O'Brien. She described meeting with Chaplin and Fairbanks concerning the director's desire to obtain backing to make two films a year for United Artists. The two men had decided that they could not afford to underwrite Lubitsch.

Indeed, United Artists was experiencing financial problems during 1923. It suffered from a lack of output on the part of its four founders – especially Griffith and Chaplin – and was at this point primarily circulating older releases, which would bring in lower rentals than new films. The firm was also still sorting out difficulties with overseas distribution. Nevertheless, Pickford suggested that some financing for Lubitsch could be solicited from outside sources. Here are some excerpts from her letter to O'Brien, written as Lubitsch was planning to move only temporarily to Warner Bros. for THE MARRIAGE CIRCLE:

> We all feel that Lubitsch would be a great asset to our company if he could do spectacles. Personally, I still believe he is the greatest director in the world and would be willing to back him if I could afford it ...
>
> Lubitsch is going to do a picture out here for a company. I am not at liberty to say which ...
>
> He is willing to take another vacation after the completion of the picture he is planning to do and start with me on January first of next year. After the completion of that picture he would want to do one or two for the United Artists. As this is a long way off there would be plenty of time to negotiate with the financial interests to secure the money for his productions. However, he wants to know if it is possible to get the money as he has several very fine offers out here, but all of them for very long term contracts, and as he is most desirous of continuing with us, he has accepted the contract to do just the one picture in order to be free when I want him again and with the possibility of doing his own productions for the United Artists ...

During June of 1923, O'Brien corresponded with Pickford, saying that he was negotiating with a newly formed company to provide at least part of the financing, but no further United Artists film by Lubitsch ever resulted.[20] There must have been a possibility of backing coming through, however, since just before ROSITA's premiere, the trade press announced that Pickford had signed a contract with Lubitsch to direct her in one film a year. The first was tenta-

tively proposed as ROMEO AND JULIET, with Douglas Fairbanks to play opposite her.[21] Even when that project faded, the friendship between the two did not
disappear, as Pickford called upon Lubitsch to help with a problem in the editing of SPARROWS in 1926; at that time she still hoped that she and Fairbanks
could work together under Lubitsch's direction.[22] All the evidence suggests
that financial problems rather than friction between star and director caused
Lubitsch to leave United Artists. Why Pickford conceived such a dislike for the
film late in her life will probably remain a mystery.

Lubitsch had in fact come to the US under contract to the Hamilton Theatrical Corporation, and hence indirectly to Famous Players-Lasky. His direction
of ROSITA had, technically, been on loan-out from FP-L. Once Lubitsch ex-
tracted himself from this contract, however, he was free to move to Warner
Bros. In mid-September, 1923, Warner Bros. announced that its original one-
film deal with Lubitsch had been changed into one in which the director
would make two "Ernst Lubitsch Productions" a year. This was the initial public announcement of THE MARRIAGE CIRCLE, which at that point had Warner
Baxter in the lead role ultimately played by Monte Blue; otherwise the cast was
the same as in the final film.[23] The director would have his own production
unit, with minimal interference from studio executives. He was free to go on
supervising the script and editing stages, as he had in Germany. Warner Bros.
gave him control over what would today be called the "final cut."[24]

In 1923, Warner Bros. had recently begun its aggressive expansion that
would eventually make it the first studio successfully to innovate sound. In
July, while it was in negotiations with Lubitsch, the company brought out the
first of a series of films with Rin-Tin-Tin; the dog had been acquired by Warner
Bros. after making three films for other companies, and he became the company's most lucrative star. Lubitsch was a more prestigious acquisition, and
the next year the ambitious studio also scored another coup by signing a contract with John Barrymore. Also late in 1924, Warner Bros. bought the first
theater in what would become an exhibition chain.[25] By the autumn of 1925,
when Warner Bros. announced its tentative release schedule for the 1926-27
season, the forty films included six specials: two by Lubitsch, two starring
Barrymore, and two with Syd Chaplin.[26] Only one of the Lubitsch specials (So
THIS IS PARIS) would be made before the director departed.

In all, Lubitsch made five films for Warner Bros. from 1924 to 1926. The
company loaned him to FP-L for FORBIDDEN PARADISE (which may have
counted as one of his two films per year). Thus he nearly fulfilled the three-
year, two-films-per-year conditions of his original contract. Despite much talk
in the trade press of further contracts to keep Lubitsch at Warner Bros., his departure from the studio apparently resulted both from the success of
Vitaphone and from the disappointing earnings of his films. In January and

February of 1926, Lubitsch had received offers from other studios and was negotiating with Warner Bros. to buy out his own contract. They in turn tried to
convince him to stay, but they felt his films were "too subtle" for audiences (a
charge corroborated by many comments from local exhibitors in the *Moving
Picture World*). Lubitsch in turn was evidently dissatisfied with the equipment
and talent that had been made available to him by the Warner Bros. studio.
When the brothers assured Lubitsch that they wanted to make bigger-budget
films aimed at the European market, the director fired back: "Am very skepti-
cal regarding your plans of bigger pictures because they require different facilities and acting material from what you have."[27]

As Lubitsch and Warners were parting ways, the firm essentially buried his
farewell film, So This Is Paris. It was released in a haphazard way at the end of
July and initially played in only a few venues. Its New York premiere came on
August 13, not in a large first-run house, but in the Cameo, a small theatre run
by the Film Arts Guild. The Cameo ordinarily ran foreign films and what today would be called "art" films. It was a prestigious place, but not one calcu-
lated to make much money or create a high profile among general exhibitors.
Indeed, the venue may have reflected the company's view that Lubitsch's
films were esoteric. Moreover, summers were traditionally a slow time for film
exhibition. *Variety*'s reviewer hinted at the oddity of this venue and of the
scheduling of a major premiere in the off-season: "A corking comedy that
should have been held back until the season. It has played some points over
the map but was first screened in New York as a preview last Friday night at
the Cameo by the Film Arts Guild. Now running there and should do business
in the small house."[28]

In August, just as So This Is Paris was making its inconspicuous way into
the market, the trade papers announced that Lubitsch had signed a long-term
contract with FP-L, which announced that "Lubitsch's contract obligations
with Warner Brothers [sic] have been fully recognized and amicably arranged."[29] Warner Bros.'s announcement of the event gave the success of
Vitaphone as the main reason for the director's departure.[30]

After a complicated set of negotiations, MGM and Paramount agreed
jointly to buy Lubitsch's Warner Bros. contract. Lubitsch would make one film
for MGM, which turned out to be The Student Prince in Old Heidelberg.
He then moved to Paramount to start a three-year contract with The Patriot,
his last fully silent film, now lost. He made another feature, Eternal Love, an
independent film distributed through United Artists. Released in 1929, it was
made in the midst of the transition to sound and was released in two versions,
silent and with a music-and-effects track. Except as an example of Lubitsch's
absorption, along with other Hollywood directors, of German techniques of

moving camera, I shall not deal with it in this book, since it was not produced fully as a silent film.

As this summary suggests, Lubitsch's Hollywood career was far more unstable than his German period. Although largely based at Warner Bros., from 1923 to 1927, he moved among studios and made films for United Artists, Famous Players-Lasky/Paramount, and MGM. Nevertheless, there was a certain continuity in the personnel with whom Lubitsch worked. Kräly continued to work on most of his scripts, and he brought costume designer Hubert to Hollywood for THE STUDENT PRINCE and THE PATRIOT. Moreover, he was able to work with casts and crews who were well steeped in the classical style of filmmaking. The consistencies of experienced collaborators in his Warner Bros. films are particularly striking.

Given Lubitsch's interest in the technical aspects of lighting, the cinematographer became an important team member. All of Lubitsch's films for Warners were photographed by Charles van Enger. Although not one of the famous cinematographers of the era, Van Enger had already had a remarkable career by 1924, when he shot THE MARRIAGE CIRCLE. He had received his first credit as recently as 1920, when he had been co-cinematographer on THE COUNTY FAIR and THE LAST OF THE MOHICANS, two films by Maurice Tourneur, the latter of which displays particularly beautiful photography. (He worked again with Tourneur in 1921 and 1923.) He also shot films for Clarence Brown, Raoul Walsh, Fred Niblo, and King Vidor, and in addition he photographed Nazimova's experimental version of SALOME in 1922. In 1924, aside from filming THE MARRIAGE CIRCLE, FORBIDDEN PARADISE, and THREE WOMEN for Lubitsch, he was the cinematographer for Victor Seastrom's first Hollywood film, NAME THE MAN. In 1925, apart from KISS ME AGAIN and LADY WINDERMERE'S FAN, he photographed THE PHANTOM OF THE OPERA. Sandwiched in among these more famous films were numerous quite ordinary projects for Warner Bros., such as a Louise Fazenda comedy, FOOTLOOSE WIDOWS (1926) and a Monte Blue railroad action picture, THE LIMITED MAIL (1925). Given such experience, it is not surprising that Van Enger was able to help Lubitsch create the precise, glowing three-point lighting on display in his Hollywood films.

Van Enger's successor, John Mescall, who was the cinematographer for So THIS IS PARIS and THE STUDENT PRINCE IN OLD HEIDELBERG, was also an old hand, though with a less distinguished resumé. He had worked on fairly ordinary films for Goldwyn from 1921 to 1923, directed by such second-stringers as Rupert Hughes and William Beaudine, as well as some films for MGM in 1924, most notably two King Vidor films, including the impressive WINE OF YOUTH. He had made numerous program pictures for Warner Bros. before working for Lubitsch, including a Rin-Tin-Tin film, a Phil Rosen melodrama, and a number of films directed by James Flood. In 1926, when he filmed So THIS IS PARIS, he was also the cinematographer on a Syd Chaplin farce, and ordinary features by Walter Morosco, William Beaudine, and Lowell Sherman.

Lubitsch films shared several crew members with other Warners films. THE MARRIAGE CIRCLE and THE LIGHTHOUSE BY THE SEA, a 1924 Rin-Tin-Tin film directed by Malcolm St. Clair, had much in common. Both had Lewis Geib and Esdras Hartley as art directors, "electrical effects" by F. N. Murphy, and art intertitles by Victor Vance. Two of the main actors in THE MARRIAGE CIRCLE formed a team during the decade. Monte Blue and Marie Prevost had starred in BRASS (released in March, 1923 and directed by Harry Rapf), with the respectable Blue marrying the flapper Prevost, who leaves him. In February, 1924, the same month when THE MARRIAGE CIRCLE appeared, an independent feature, DAUGHTERS OF PLEASURE (directed by William Beaudine) was released; in it, Blue played a womanizing cad trying to seduce flapper Prevost and ending by marrying her. In July, BEING RESPECTABLE, by Phil Rosen had Blue as a husband in a loveless marriage nearly lured away by old flame Prevost but opting for respectability. In September Warners released Harry Beaumont's THE LOVER OF CAMILLE, with Blue as an actor who has an affair with Prevost and is jilted by her. In 1925, Lubitsch's KISS ME AGAIN paired them as a married couple, with Prevost tempted to stray. That same year saw Harry Beaumont directing them as true lovers in RECOMPENSE for Warner Bros., and they co-starred one last time in 1927, in Erle C. Kenton's OTHER WOMEN'S HUSBANDS, a comedy with a plot somewhat similar to that of So THIS IS PARIS, with the straying husband trying to seduce his own wife at a costume ball.

In short, Lubitsch did not enter the Hollywood system without support. At Warner Bros., he worked in an environment of established genres and with people experienced in the emerging classical style. His films fit into familiar patterns, but they would soar miles above nearly anything else in a system predicated on cranking out romantic comedies and costume dramas.

Lubitsch's Reputation in the 1920s

By coincidence, Lubitsch arrived in America at the end of 1922, the year when Griffith made his last really successful major film, ORPHANS OF THE STORM (the New York premiere of which Lubitsch had attended during his first New York stay). It must have been galling to the great American pioneer to see Lubitsch dubbed the "European Griffith" and then to watch him steal the critical limelight. Before Lubitsch arrived in Hollywood, Griffith had enjoyed the reputation as the father of the movies and as the young art-form's pre-eminent director. As the 1920s progressed, Lubitsch seems to have rapidly taken over Griffith's position, with the revered older director receding to a more grandfatherly status.

Supposedly the "European Griffith" sobriquet was coined in an article in *Motion Picture Magazine* in February of 1921, shortly after the American premiere of MADAME DUBARRY (aka PASSION).[31] An important 1922 story in *Photoplay* referred to Lubitsch as "The German film wizard, master of tragedy, and the man who makes history live," and drew upon what was already a stock phrase: "'The Griffith of Europe,' sometimes called, because of the genius with which he made 'Passion,' 'Deception,' and 'The Loves of Pharaoh.'"[32] The famous *Variety* review that attributed the film to "Emil Subitsch" (supposedly in response to an attempt to conceal the film's German origins) also praised this unknown filmmaker, who "made the story his first consideration, subordinating everything else. This is great direction." The same reviewer commented that "The direction holds points of interest for all professions."[33] The idea that Lubitsch, as a foreign director, could provide a model for his Hollywood counterparts was established early on.

Lubitsch's reputation grew stratospherically during the 1920s. As Eyman points out, he was the only director to figure on all of the first five *Film Daily* lists of the ten best directors.[34] When Lubitsch signed with Famous Players-Lasky in 1926, the *Moving Picture World* described him in exalted terms: "The man whose sheer genius catapulted him to the peak of film fame, first in Europe and then in America."[35] After Lubitsch had finished LADY WINDERMERE'S FAN in 1925, the *Moving Picture World* pointed out: "It will be remembered that the picture rights to this drama were long sought after unsuccessfully by film producers, and the trustees of Oscar Wilde's estate finally gave their consent to its screening only when assured that the direction would be in the hands of Lubitsch."[36]

In early 1926, the Film Arts Guild held a two-week retrospective of Lubitsch's films at the Cameo Theatre in New York. (Ironically, in August, as we have seen, the Cameo would be the venue for Warners' low-key premiere of SO THIS IS PARIS.) Such a showing of the work of a single director, in this case including mostly Lubitsch's Hollywood films and MADAME DUBARRY, was considered a first.[37] The release of THE STUDENT PRINCE IN OLD HEIDELBERG elicited plaudits beyond what one would expect for a good but hardly extraordinary film: "Made by a German director who stands foremost in the ranks of the elect."[38] Even a lukewarm review in the *Brooklyn Eagle* gushed over Lubitsch himself:

Ernst Lubitsch is, of course, a director of deserved international repute. Upon his past records, which include such brilliant photoplays as "Passion," "The Marriage

Circle," and "Forbidden Paradise," he stands seemingly at the head of his class on the Camera Coast. The very presence of his name among the credit titles of a picture is enough to start even the most judicious film reporters scrambling for their dictionaries in feverish search of superlative adjectives. In the eyes of his palpitating admirers (and his admirers are very nearly legion) this king of the megaphonists can do no wrong.[39]

Actor John Loder, a friend of Lubitsch's, summarized his reputation in 1932:

> If you moved in Hollywood studio circles you would quickly realize that by people who really know the facts Lubitsch is regarded with admiration – amounting almost to veneration – that is almost unique. There is hardly a star in Hollywood who would not think it a privilege – and would acknowledge the fact with humility – to be directed by this astonishing little German. There is scarcely a director who is not prepared to "take off his hat" to "the Master."[40]

The year before, Griffith had made his last film, THE STRUGGLE.

Despite the fact that Lubitsch's films were considered a bit too sophisticated to be really big money-makers, his salary was apparently the highest of any director in Hollywood in the mid-1920s. A 1926 memo compiled at Universal listed Lubitsch as receiving $175,000 per film, far above even the second highest, Erich Von Stroheim, at $100,000 per film. The next highest was $50,000 per film, earned by James Cruze, Alan Dwan, George Fitzmaurice, and Henry King, and many directors were paid by the week, typically $1000 to $2000.[41] Germany's top director had become, arguably, Hollywood's top director. I turn now to an examination of how such a thing could happen.

Areas of Stylistic Influence

To start to answer this question, we need to chart how stylistic influences passed from American cinema to German cinema in the immediate postwar years (Chapters Two to Five) and later moved from German cinema to Hollywood (Chapter Six). Despite historians' concentration on the *enfesselte* camera and its adoption in American films in the second half of the 1920s, the American influence on Germany was far more pervasive and important, and it will receive the bulk of the attention.

Lubitsch can be seen as both an emblem of these influences and a conduit for them. His extraordinary grasp of film technique meant that he was the most proficient practitioner, initially of the post-war German stylistic norms, and latterly of the new tendencies that became apparent as Hollywood films came into the country. Those tendencies show up in his films before they do in the work of other German directors. Lubitsch's quick adoption of classical Hollywood norms, however, also helped accustom other German filmmakers to these new ideas. We shall see a number of instances where industry commentators cited Lubitsch's films as exemplary of how American techniques could be taken up in German filmmaking.

I have chosen four areas of style in which to seek evidence of influences moving from the US to Germany. Techniques of the silent era fall into the general areas of cinematography, editing, mise-en-scene. For my purposes, I have narrowed cinematography down to lighting (which is, strictly speaking, an aspect of mise-en-scene, but which is in practice largely handled by the cinematographer). The moving camera was not a particularly important aspect of German films in the immediate post-war era. Similarly, German cinema does not use framing in a particularly distinctive way until the adoption of analytical editing, where a greater variety of framings is used. Thus framing will be more relevant in Chapter Four, when editing is discussed. Editing in general was a major factor in Hollywood's influence, since German filmmakers recognized and began to adhere to the newly-formulated continuity guidelines. The two main components of mise-en-scene, setting and acting, are important enough to warrant separate chapters of their own.

Chapters Two through Five are arranged beginning with the most concretely demonstrable area of influence and moving toward the least. Influences in lighting are relatively easy to trace, because they depend on various types of lamps and their systematic arrangements. The resulting arrangements are often fairly easy for the analyst to detect in the finished images on the screen. Moreover, because of the complexity of lighting, practitioners tend to write about it in technical journals directed at filmmakers, and these occasionally contain diagrams of normative lighting plans. Influences in set design and editing are perhaps somewhat more difficult to detect and prove, but again, the practitioners sometimes write articles about their assumptions, and one can trace consistent usage across a group of films. By contrast, editing does not depend on a specific technology, and discussions of it appear in the contemporary professional literature only rarely. Patterns of cutting, however, can be discerned systematically through analysis of many specific sequences. Acting is undoubtedly the most elusive of the areas of film style I shall deal with here, since performances styles vary so much among individual actors and different genres. Once we have examined the strong concrete evidence for influence in areas like lighting and set design, however, the idea that other areas like acting also were subject to parallel influences becomes more plausible. As I have mentioned, camera movement famously became important in Germany in mid-1920s with the popularization of the *enfesselte* camera, which I will deal with separately in Chapter Six, in the context of a broader discussion of the

German-American exchange of stylistic influences of the mid- to late-1920s –
after Lubitsch's transition to Hollywood filmmaking. Indeed, as we shall see
in that chapter, Lubitsch himself only began using fluid camera movements to
a significant extent when he, along with other Hollywood directors, saw German
films using the *enfesselte* camera in the mid-1920s.

I shall end with a brief discussion of the origins of that cliché invariably in-
voked in writings about the director, "the Lubitsch touch," and of what the
phrase might have meant during the 1920s.

2 Making the Light Come from the Story: Lighting

Different Lighting Equipment

Lubitsch's lighting style changed noticeably between his German features made up to 1921 and the two he directed for Paramount in Berlin. It changed again after he went to Hollywood in 1922. Lubitsch's move to the US came at a crucial point in the history of lighting in the two countries, both in terms of the actual technology and of approaches to the placement of equipment in the sets. American lighting styles had undergone major developments from 1915 to 1919, primarily via the proliferation of dark-studio shooting, which replaced sunlight with artificial illumination. Specifically, studios increasingly relied on small arc spotlights and high-powered arcs suitable for night shooting. During the late 1910s, American production companies were depending less on the traditional flat overall illumination provided by sunlight, floodlighting, or a combination of the two. Studio filmmaking turned increasingly to selective lighting, especially back-lighting.

Before the war, European filmmaking technology had generally been parallel to that of American studios. During the war years, however, Germany was largely out of touch with developments in lighting equipment. Over the period when Lubitsch made many of his German films, the studios there were a few years behind the Americans, using lamps designed for flat, frontal lighting.

Lubitsch himself commented on the difference between American and German lighting possibilities. Shortly after he had finished THE MARRIAGE CIRCLE in late 1923, he published an article comparing American and German cinematography. He emphasized the varied equipment he found in America:

> The American technique of lighting is different from the system used abroad. It is far more elaborate and thanks to the superiority of American technical equipment, surpasses anything I have seen before. I don't know yet how many different lights the American cinematographer has at his disposal. We in Berlin were very proud of our few spot lights and had no idea of the variety of spots you Americans have, from the "baby spots" for small surfaces to those large, powerful fountains of light, the giant spots. There is something for every contingency and each imaginable situation.[1]

Lubitsch singles out the variety of spotlights as a significant difference between the German and American studios. Such spots were to be an important basis for the changes in the look of his films. By comparing German and American lighting technology in the late 1910s and early 1920s, we can pinpoint one reason why Lubitsch's lighting style changes so greatly in the early 1920s-and why other German filmmakers more gradually adopted the norms established in Hollywood.[2]

Most of the earliest film studios in all producing countries were glass-sided, allowing sunlight to pass through the walls and provide the main source of light. Often tiny prisms in the glass diffused the sunlight so that it did not create dark, sharp-edged shadows. In some cases, supplementary artificial light was used. During the late 1910s, American film companies increasingly built "dark" studios: large buildings with solid walls and few or no windows. The adoption of completely artificial light allowed for flexibility and control over illumination. Outside the US, most film firms continued to use glass studios into the 1920s.

From an early period, some production companies – mainly in the US – had used artificial light to supplement or replace daylight. Most early equipment was designed to simulate full sunshine, in that it consisted of floodlights, which provided sheets of light over broad areas of a set. Because multiple lamps were usually used, however, the light was far more diffuse than unfiltered daylight. Undiffused sunlight cast a single deep, sharply-outlined shadow behind each object, while multiple floodlights tended to soften or even eliminate each other's shadows. Spotlights, like sunlight, could create a sharp shadow behind an object, but unlike sunlight, they concentrated intense light on only one portion of a set. Spotlights came into general usage later than floodlights.

One of the most popular devices for creating diffused lighting was the mercury-vapor tube, made by Cooper-Hewitt, a division of Westinghouse (Fig. 2.1). These tubes were usually mounted in groups on floor stands or overhead units angled into the acting area; both types are shown in this 1909 image of the Biograph Studio in New York. The Germans imported mercury-vapors from the US beginning before World War I, since they were the only major type of lighting device in use which was not manufactured in Germany. (Domestic mercury-vapors began being produced only in 1926.) Figures 2.2 and 2.3 are German cinematography-manual illustrations, showing an upright floor unit and a hanging unit.[3]

A second type of flood lighting was provided by arc lamps. These could be of two types. The first is an open floor-stand unit, as in the example at the lower left in Figure 2.4, which shows American models of lighting equipment.[4] The second type of arc light is a hanging lamp in a glass enclosure; the one shown at the upper left in Figure 2.4 has a funnel-shaped reflector and was designed to hang directly above the set. Both these lamps were made by the Wohl company in America. The light each one produced was diffuse rather than concentrated in the manner of a spotlight. Germany produced very similar units, such as the portable floor-stand model shown in Figure 2.5, made by Weinert (along with Jupiter and Efa, one of the main German manufacturers of film-lighting equipment). Note here especially the double set of carbon arcs; as we shall see, these could create strange and distracting shadows in a film image. Figure 2.6 shows the same company's hanging arc, a type of lamp that provides flat overhead light. In Figure 2.7, John Collins directs THE CHILDREN OF EVE (1915) at the Edison studio; overhead is a bank of glass-enclosed arcs, each mounted with a slanted reflector to direct the light into the set. Figure 2.8 shows a group of similar lamps, made by Weinert in Germany, arranged on a floor stand so as to cast a bright, even light into a set from the front or side. A production photograph (Fig. 2.9) shows the interior of the JOFA-Atelier in Berlin in 1920. As with most glass studios in Germany, electric light was available to supplement sunlight when the weather was overcast or for filming early or late in the day.

Unlike floodlights, spotlights could focus a beam of concentrated light on a relatively small area; a single spot created a dark, sharp-edged shadow somewhat comparable to that cast by sunshine. The carbon-arc spotlight came into general use in Hollywood in the mid-1910s. Figure 2.10 shows a 1920s group of the famous Kliegl spots (called klieg lights). The Germans had similar devices, made domestically, as with the Jupiter-brand unit in Figure 2.11. This is probably the sort of thing Lubitsch refers to in the passage quoted above, when he speaks of being "very proud of our few spot lights."

World War I created a lag in German lighting technology, and Lubitsch was well aware of the difference. In his 1923 article comparing German and American cinematographers, he asked:

> Are the German cinematographers in the same class as the Americans? I shall answer: Yes, as far as their ability goes – but they haven't had the time nor the technical equipment to develop their art to so high a degree. The years of the war were an entire loss to German cinematography, and even during the years following the war there was the handicap of money stringency and economic stress.[5]

In his 1927 cinematography manual *Der praktische Kameraman*, Guido Seeber describes how during the war even the practice of using mercury-vapor lamps was set back because it was impossible to get replacement tubes from America. More importantly, the Germans were at least two years behind the American companies in the introduction of giant arcs and in the general move into large studios lit entirely by artificial light. In early 1918, the Sunlight Arc Company started supplying Hollywood firms with a high-intensity lamp of the type developed for military searchlights during the war (Fig. 2.12). Three or four such lamps could light a large exterior set at night, and as a result, night-for-night shooting increased after 1918. These large spots were also used as supplemental light during daytime shooting out of doors, as in Figure 2.13, where a First National team films TOPSY AND EVA (1927). With sunlight arcs, large sets could be built in darkened studios, and this became a major trend in Hollywood beginning in the late 1910s.

Comparable "sunlight" spots did not come into use in Germany until 1920, when Weinert brought out a relatively small unit. Larger units (Fig. 2.14) appeared during the next two years. In 1926, Seeber described the change: "Primarily intended for high-level military and maritime technical applications, searchlights had a significance for cinematography only when it was decided to create effects, because the light always shines on only a limited area."[6] By "effects," Seeber means selective, concentrated light motivated as coming from a specific source within the scene, as opposed to a diffused, flat light. During the 1920s, German production firms followed the American example by building large dark studios.

Although such efforts eventually narrowed the technological gap, it seems very likely that Germany's brief lag after the war was a major cause of the distinctly different lighting styles in films from the two countries.

Different Conceptions of Lighting

Even more important, however, was the fact that by the War's end, German filmmakers had very different notions about where to place their lights than did their American counterparts. The lighting layout for most shots was arranged so as simply to make everything *visible*. Walls, actors, furniture, props, all received an overall, diffuse light, usually coming from the front and top. The notion of creating atmosphere, depth, modeling, and other effects through lighting was distinctly secondary. Figure 2.15 is an overhead lighting plot given in Hans Schmidt's 1921 manual, the *Kino-Taschenbuch*, as an "artistic" way to illuminate a film stage. The camera at the left faces a backdrop, B. The line marked F shows the front of the area of staged action, while R is an overhead railing for hanging lights. The asterisks 1-6 are floodlights on floor stands, while 7 and 8 represent floodlights hanging above the action. The lamps can typically be either arc floodlights or sets of mercury-vapors. Either provides diffuse, bright light, though arc light tends to be harsher and somewhat more concentrated. Two things are immediately apparent. The light comes entirely from the front and top, with no hint of back-lighting, and the light is generally balanced, although Schmidt suggests that to create shadows, the filmmaker can turn down the lamps on one side.[7] We can call this basic layout the V-pattern of lighting. Cases where the lights on both sides are turned on will be a balanced V-pattern, while cases where light comes from only one side will be an unbalanced V-pattern. In many cases, the light provided by lamps arranged in this fashion merely supplemented the diffused daylight that came through the studios' glass walls. We have already seen this in the JOFA Studios (Figure 2.9). Figures 2.16 and 2.17 show the Union (PAGU) glass studio, where Lubitsch shot most of his German features.

Post-War German films by Lubitsch and other directors confirm that the V-pattern of lamp arrangement and the diffuse illumination that results dominate the standard practices of the era. It was an approach that had been employed without much modification since the early 1910s. German films certainly do use occasional lighting effects to simulate lamps or fireplaces, and occasional shots with back-lighting appear. In general, though, German filmmakers depended on floodlighting. That is, as we have seen, most of the light pouring into the set is diffuse and of equal brightness on both settings and actors. This same approach was in widespread in use in other European countries as well. It was essentially comparable to the way Hollywood films had been lit in the period from roughly 1912 to 1915, but which American filmmakers would have considered old-fashioned only a few years later.

During the mid-1910s to the early 1920s, Hollywood practitioners were developing a distinctive style called three-point lighting. The basic principle behind this approach was that the lighting used in a set could be made darker or brighter in different areas in order to guide the viewer's attention to those parts of the action most salient to understanding the ongoing story. The primary, or *key*, light would typically concentrate on the main actors. The setting, which might be rather busy in its design and hence might draw the eye away from the actors, would be lit with a somewhat dimmer, or *fill*, light. A slightly darker set would create a sense of greater depth when the brightly-lit actors stood in front of it. Fill light could also be cast on the actors from the side opposite the key light, softening shadows and creating an attractive, modeled look. Finally, the third point of the system was *back-lighting*. Lamps could be placed on the tops of the sets at the rear or directed through windows or other openings in the sets; these would project highlights onto the actors' hair and trace a little outline of light around their bodies, often termed "edge" light. The combination of these three types of light could yield an attractive image in which light unobtrusively aided the telling of a story. After looking at some diagrams of how the lamps were typically arranged around the set, we shall look at some examples of how the results looked on the screen.

Consider some American equivalents of the lighting plot shown in Figure 2.15. Figure 2.18 was displayed in 1919 during a presentation to the Society of Motion Picture Engineers, an American professional association dedicated to standardizing many aspects of film technology. This plot reveals a very different approach from that of the Germans. The camera faces obliquely into an L-shaped set. (Overhead lights are not shown in the plot, although they would be used.) Most strikingly, three large arc floodlights pour light in from one side. Each has a reflector placed beside it, sending part of the light slightly back toward the camera. Two small optional arcs behind the set can be used to focus back-light through openings in the walls such as windows or doors. Virtually none of the light is coming directly from the front, and more light comes from one side than from the other.[8] That is, the bright side provides the key illumination, the dimmer side the fill.

Figure 2.19 is a plot for a simpler box set, made in 1923, the year Lubitsch began working in Hollywood.[9] Here the elaborate lighting from all sides, with its careful combination of several sorts of lighting instruments, is apparent. The camera is at the bottom of the diagram. At the rear of the set, two pairs of 75-amp spotlights are placed at the corners, aiming diagonally down into the set (A). Between them is a row of four smaller, 25- or 50-amp spotlights (B). All three walls have four small carbon-arc floodlights arrayed along the top (C). Overhead there are two hanging units of mercury-vapor tubes (D) and two large ceiling lamps (G). The camera is flanked on either side by two multiple-tube mercury-vapor units arranged in a V on either side of the camera (E); these in turn have more small arc floods arranged in the spaces between them (C). There is a huge arc lamp (presumably a sunlight arc) at the lower left, somewhat removed from all the others (F), and finally, a baby spot just to the right of the camera provides an additional light for any actor who approaches the camera.

How this complex array of lamps yields three-point lighting is evident. The key light comes from the left, created by the large arc and the other units on the left side of the set. The right-hand side, without a large arc, provides a somewhat softer fill light. No fewer than *twelve* lamps are devoted to providing the back-lighting, guaranteeing that any actor can move about the set and still appear to glow with an outline of edge light. Thus, although the V of mercury-vapors on either side of the camera may superficially resemble that of our German lighting plot, the addition of specific directional lights at the side and rear creates a very different illumination.

Such complicated arrays of lamps are difficult to convey in production photographs taken on the sets of Hollywood films. A still of the FP-L production of THE CAREER OF KATHERINE BUSH (1919) shows the filming taking place inside a dark studio, lit entirely by artificial light (Fig. 2.20). The original caption for this image describes it in this way: "There are no overhead lights in this set except such as come from the upper banks of the Cooper-Hewitt [i.e., mercury-vapor lamps] 'Goose-Necks.' Between the Cooper-Hewitt banks may be seen several Kleigel [i.e., Kliegl or klieg] flood lights and at the back three spot-lights to give back-lighting."[10]

In Figure 2.21, a set from circa 1925 shows a layout fairly similar to the plot shown in Figure 2.19.[11] There are mercury-vapors and floods visible at the front and sides, as well as a spotlight in the foreground right; it may have been used to create a highlight on a specific object. Note also two banks of mercury-vapors above and toward the back, angled toward the front, as well as a row of spotlights on top of the rear wall. These could provide a fairly intense edge lighting.

What results did such lighting layouts produce on the screen? For one thing, the use of directional arc lighting could create selective illumination. In a 1925 lecture to the Society of Motion Picture Engineers, the publicity photo from ROBIN HOOD in Figure 2.22 was described as "an excellent example of artistic utilization of light revealing the magnitude and depth of this elaborate setting."[12] Rather than a flat, frontal wash of light, the cinematographer has aimed lamps to cast brighter pools of illumination over portions of the scene. Such selective lighting could create atmosphere and beauty, and, more importantly, could isolate figures against less obtrusive backgrounds. Note here how the tiny figure running up the steps is centered in the main area of light.

One way in which light could set the figures apart was by emphasizing their three-dimensionality. The same 1925 lecture demonstrated the importance of edge lighting. In the top image of Figure 2.23, three actors with dark hair or clothes are placed against a partially black background.[13] The highlights on both men's hair, on the central man's sleeve, and on the woman's shoulder, pick their outlines out against the darkness. In the lower still, the highlights have been blotted out, showing how crucial is the modeling provided by the strips of edge lighting. As we shall see, this sort of back-lighting was not a part of German film style until after Hollywood films began to influence filmmakers.

The effect of back-lighting is obvious in American films of the late 1910s and early 1920s. In THE GHOST OF ROSIE TAYLOR (1918), for example, back-lighting makes the heroine's hair glow and sets her off starkly from the darker background (Fig. 2.24). From the early 1910s on, Hollywood filmmakers routinely used reflectors on location to soften shadows with fill light, especially on faces. In another scene from THE GHOST OF ROSIE TAYLOR (Fig. 2.25), the sun shines into the scene from above and slightly behind the actors, yet the broad-rimmed hat worn by the woman on the right causes no difficulty for our seeing her face clearly; one or more reflectors have cast sunlight onto it. By the early 1920s, back-lighting was in nearly universal use in America, and it was perhaps the technique that attracted the most immediate attention among German filmmakers.

Lubitsch and the German Norm

As we have seen, the most basic lighting set-up in German filmmaking of the 1910s was the V-pattern, creating diffused, overall lighting from the front and top. A medium-long shot from MR. WU (Fig. 2.26, 1918) demonstrates the effect of this set-up in a typical scene. Note the slight shadow down the center of the woman's face, indicating the fact that no lamps have been placed directly in front of the scene, that is, in or very near the space occupied by the camera. We shall see more dramatic results of this gap in the lighting shortly. Figure 2.27, from DIE BRÜDER KARAMASSOFF (1920) shows diffused sunlight over the entire scene, with artificial light coming from above to highlight the actresses' hair and perhaps additional light from lamps on either side of the camera.

Lubitsch's use of this standard lighting lay-out is dramatically evident in Figure 2.28, from DIE PUPPE. The diffused illumination here is provided entirely by artificial lighting. The large mercury-vapor floor-stand units, placed to either side of the camera in the standard V-pattern, are reflected in the shiny metal containers stacked on the shelves at the center rear. The fact that the lamps to the right of the camera are slightly brighter than those to the left is evident in three ways: in the reflections, in the fact that the actor at the left casts a dim shadow on the wall, and in the shadow cast by the nose and cheek of the actor at the right. The same effect could result from banks of arc floodlights, as is apparent in KOHLHIESELS TÖCHTER (Fig. 2.29), where the white dots in the small pot on the table reflect the clusters of lamps. The bright unit slightly to the left casts the actor's shadow on the wall to the right of him, while the right-hand unit, placed further to the side and closer to the table, creates shadows on his face and a highlight on the set to the left of him.

With SUMURUN, we have a rare chance to compare a shot from one of Lubitsch's films to a production photograph showing a lighting set-up for what is evidently the same scene. Figure 2.30 shows Lubitsch filming Paul Wegener in a throne-room set.[14] Most of the illumination is sunlight, coming from the upper right directly down on the action. Floor-stand arcs are aimed into the scene, also from right to left. There is no evidence of back-light, and indeed a shot from the film itself made in this same set (Fig. 2.31) shows a bright, harsh sunlight illuminating the actors from slightly to the right of the camera; there is no indication that the arc lights seen in the production photograph were used for this shot.

The unbalanced V-pattern also appears quite frequently in post-War German films. In Figure 2.32, from MR. WU, bright light floods the scene only from the left – sunlight, to judge from the reflection in the chair. Although the light is diffuse enough to illuminate the actor's neck, the left side of his face is largely cast in shadow. A Hollywood film from the same year would be likely to add fill light to soften such a shadow. LANDSTRASSE UND GROSSSTADT (1921, Fig. 2.33), uses sunlight from the left, apparently with some supplementary top light, resulting in very heavily shadowed areas.

Lubitsch uses this approach as well, often lighting the scene from only one side of the V-pattern. In CARMEN (Fig. 2.34), the presence of the prison wall extending into depth at the right makes the use of lamps on that side impossible, so sunlight is directed in from the left front (with the grid of the glass studio walls visible in the helmet). In this shot from DIE AUSTERNPRINZESSIN, a wash of arc lighting comes from the foreground left against a flat back wall, as evidenced by the shadows on the set at the right and the glare in the picture at the left. Not all such shots were as starkly and heavily shadowed as these examples. Lubitsch uses side and top light in MADAME DUBARRY (Fig. 2.36) to create a nicely modeled two-shot.

German filmmakers did depart from the V-pattern at times, sometimes creating quite lovely images. This scene from ROSE BERND (Fig. 2.37, 1919) shows a corridor scene shot against the sun, yielding edge light on the men beyond the arch and a range of dark and light areas in the foreground. Lubitsch used this tactic now and then, as in SUMURUN (Fig. 2.38), where the fact that the scene is a night interior makes dark shadows on the characters desirable. Here sunlight was the sole source, but artificial back-light appears in ANNA BOLEYN (Fig. 2.39), coming from arcs hidden behind the set and angled through the open door.

The notion of placing lamps on the top of the set to create back-lighting seems not, however, to have occurred to the Germans. As the three examples above show, one method of creating back-lighting was simply to place a doorway or frame of some sort in the middle ground and light the space beyond more brightly than the foreground. This happens more obviously in DIE LIEBSCHAFTEN DES HEKTOR DALMORE (1921; Fig. 2.40), where the brightly lit rear room creates silhouettes when characters pass through the door. Lubitsch uses a similar effect in a prison scene in CARMEN (Fig. 2.41), where he also aims dim diffused light in through the windows at the right, creating a fairly elaborate lighting scheme for the period.

In rare cases, genuine edge lighting appears, often created by having considerable top lighting that extends beyond the actor. Such edge light tends to occur in relatively close shots, such as this tight framing of the heroine in DIE EHE DER FÜRSTIN DEMIDOFF (1921, Fig. 2.42), which very much resembles the sort of glamour shots being made in Hollywood during the late 1910s. Although most shots in DIE BRÜDER KARAMASSOF do not contain edge lighting, there are occasional exceptions (Fig. 2.43).

From about 1912 on, American films increasingly used lighting "effects," shots in which a source within the story space provides the light-at least ostensibly. German films did the same thing after the war, as in this shot from MR. WU (Fig. 2.44), where the scene's light supposedly comes entirely from the lamp at the left, or this from DER WEISSE PFAU (1920, Fig. 2.45), where an arc lamp simulates firelight. Lubitsch creates a beautiful shot in MADAME DUBARRY using only top-light from an offscreen lamp presumed to be hanging over the revolutionaries' table (Fig. 2.46). As early as DIE AUGEN DER MUMIE MÂ, Lubitsch picks out the heroine's onstage dance with a moving spotlight (Fig. 2.47). It is presumably one of the "few spot lights" Lubitsch referred to in the *American Cinematographer* article quoted above.

Effects lighting is a specific type of selective lighting, that is, lighting cast over only part of the space to be filmed. In general, selective lighting departs considerably from the overall, diffused illumination typical of the V-pattern. As the examples just given suggest, selective lighting tended to be used for night interiors. Despite his adherence to the V-pattern in most circumstances, Lubitsch occasionally made original and dramatic use of selective lighting. In MADAME DUBARRY, for example, when Jeanne hears her lover and the other revolutionaries plotting against the king, her face is initially lit to display her shocked expression (Fig. 2.48), but as she backs away to leave surreptitiously, she becomes a silhouette against the lighter background wall, with its small effects lamp (Fig. 2.49).

So the German system of lighting had some flexibility – but by Hollywood standards, it also had many problems. Some of these problems no doubt became apparent to German filmmakers as soon as American films were again allowed into the country. Lubitsch, with his technical knowledge and particular interest in lighting, would have been more sensitive to such "flaws" than most.

In some cases, German (and most European) filmmakers simply went on using techniques that had been standard since before the war. One of the most obvious instances is the continued building of sets representing interiors – sometimes constructed in glass studios, sometime outdoors – but lit with bright daylight. This ballroom setting in I.N.R.I.: DIE KATASTROPHE EINES VOLKES (1920, Fig. 2.50) is reminiscent of the comparable set in Griffith's INTOLERANCE, which was already beginning to look a bit old-fashioned for a Hollywood film from 1916. A theater lobby in DER WEISSE PFAU (Fig. 2.51) gets the same treatment. Lubitsch's films contain many examples, perhaps none so obvious and (again by American norms) so outdated as the huge open-air cathedral set in ANNA BOLEYN (Fig. 2.52).

A more pervasive difficulty created specifically by the V-pattern was distracting shadows on the sets. With no fill light to soften or erase these shadows, they could be simple and stark in a small set and simply multiply in a large set. In ROSE BERND, a room crammed with game trophies and other items hanging on the wall becomes even busier when each casts at least one conspicuous shadow (Fig. 2.53). This is an extreme example, but actors often cast distracting shadows on the sets, as in DER WEISSE PFAU (Fig. 2.54). Lubitsch's films are prone to this problem, as in KOHLHIESELS TÖCHTER (Fig. 2.55).

The example in Figure 2.54 displays a type of shadow typical in German post-War films. One of the most commonly used lighting instruments was the small floor-stand arc with two pairs of carbons side by side (see Figure 2.5). When placed fairly close to an actor and used without any fill light on the set, such a lamp cast a shadow with a second, fainter shadow along its edges. Such shadows are exemplified by simple compositions from NERVEN (1919; Fig. 2.56) and DIE EHE DER FÜRSTIN DEMIDOFF (Fig. 2.57). Lubitsch's films are full of similar shadows, as shots from ROMEO UND JULIA IM SCHNEE (Fig. 2.58) and DIE BERGKATZE (Fig. 2.59) demonstrate. Eye-catching shadows cast by arc lights are so widespread in German post-War films that we must assume that practitioners did not perceive them as a problem and felt no need to attempt to eliminate them by adding fill light. The V-pattern remained the norm.

The lack of fill light is noticeable in films shot on location as well. In Hollywood, the employment of reflectors involved no prohibitively complex or expensive technology; most of them were simply sheets of wood painted white or covered with light-colored canvas. German filmmakers, however, seem not to have used them. In a scene shot at a small country fair in ROSE BERND, the faces of the actors are almost obscured by shadow, in particular the one cast by the man's hat (Fig. 2.60); to many modern eyes, the effect is probably quite charming visually, but it would not pass muster in the American studios of the era. Lubitsch's films take the same approach, and the faces of people with visors or hat rims almost disappear, as in CARMEN (Fig. 2.61) and DIE AUGEN DER MUMIE MÂ (Fig. 2.62).

A somewhat similar problem arose from the almost complete avoidance of back-lighting. One of the main purposes of back-lighting was to ensure a separation of the actor from the set, emphasizing the depth of space and focusing the main attention on the actors as the carriers of narrative information. Without back-lighting, actors might sometimes even blend distractingly into settings, especially when dark hair and clothes were juxtaposed with dark backgrounds, as Figures 2.63 and 2.64, from MEYER AUS BERLIN and ROMEO UND JULIA IM SCHNEE, suggest.

The V-pattern caused two other distinctive effects: harsh glare and what I shall rather ominously call "the dark zone." Both of these effects had been eliminated by the formulation of three-point lighting in Hollywood, and they would have seemed outdated and clumsy to practitioners there.

When artificial light was primarily used to illuminate an entire set, the lamps had to cast a bright wash over the entire area. Since that wash came from the front, shiny objects in the set often reflected the light, creating what could be considered a distracting glare – especially when opening and closing doors flashed such a reflection only briefly, as often happened. Hardly a door gets opened in these German films without a momentary glimpse of this kind of glare, as when the heroine opens a cupboard in ROSE BERND (Fig. 2.65) or an assistant enters an office in LANDSTRASSE UND GROSSSTADT (Fig. 2.66). Again, Lubitsch's German work follows the norm. The shiny outer door of the doll shop in DIE PUPPE picks up the bright light from just off right front (Fig. 2.67). Shiny furniture creates the same sort of glare, as with the chairs at left and right in a shot from MADAME DUBARRY (Fig. 2.68).

Looking back at the German lighting plot in Figure 2.15, we can see that the V-pattern leaves a gap at the point of the V where no lamp can apparently be placed because the camera occupies that space. One American solution, as shown in Figure 2.19, was to place a small, or "Baby" spotlight close beside the camera to illuminate the faces of any actors who might need to move into the foreground. Instead or additionally, a reflector might be held or propped against the tripod, bouncing back-light up into faces. As with fill light, German filmmakers apparently did not think it necessary to do anything about this dark zone.

The dark zone would not be a problem if actors never approached the camera. The Germans, however, had not given up the somewhat outmoded practice of having actors exit and enter diagonally just to the side of the camera. (Diagonal movements of this sort did not disappear entirely from Hollywood films; both Lubitsch and Tod Browning used them during the 1920s.) Such exits and entrances brought them into the dark zone. In a party scene in MR. WU, for example, a young man moving out on the left of the camera suddenly passes into an area where his face is in shadow (Fig. 2.69). One scene in DIE LIEBSCHAFTEN DES HEKTOR DALMORE has the actors at a distance, in standard V-pattern light (Fig. 2.70), but when Dalmore moves forward to exit to the left, he suddenly encounters a patch of darkness just in front of the camera (Fig. 2.71).

Lubitsch seems to have been fond of these to-camera movements, for nearly all of his German features have scenes that bring actors into the dark zone. In MADAME DUBARRY, the revolutionary walks along a hallway lit from both sides, passing a patch of bright arc illumination from off right (Fig. 2.72); note the double shadow cast by the chair at the rear, also lit in the V-pattern. As he moves forward, he passes out of the bright arc light and into an area with no lamps at all on the right, only on the left (Fig. 2.73). Finally he approaches the camera and passes into an area not illuminated at all (Fig. 2.74). The same sort of thing can happen with the unbalanced V-pattern, as when the capitalist walks along a hallway in DIE AUSTERNPRINZESSIN. A bright arc off left illuminates him and the wall, casting the characteristic shadow of the double-carbon arc (Fig. 2.75); as he moves in front of the camera, he passes almost entirely into shadow (Fig. 2.76).

Germany's Discovery of Three-point Lighting

When American films finally showed openly in Germany at the beginning of 1921, the reaction to the new Hollywood style was one of delighted astonishment. The unfamiliar methods of three-point lighting, especially back-lighting, seem to have been especially impressive to industry practitioners and commentators.

Among the important Hollywood films shown after the ban ended was the first new Mary Pickford feature, DADDY-LONG-LEGS. It was trade-shown in Berlin in February and provided a dramatic demonstration of three-point lighting. The *Lichtbildbühne*'s reviewer praised the clarity of the script and Pickford's performance. The most interesting aspect of the film was, he declared, the technique: "The amazing achievement of depth effects [*Tiefenwirkungen*] as much as the illumination of the images of the characters (surely produced with the aid of mirrors) and the wonderfully clean special effects."[15] The "depth effects" referred to here are almost certainly the back-lighting, which, as we have seen, tends to separate the actor from the background. Back-lighting had the added advantage of creating a glamorous effect for Pickford (Fig. 2.77). Shots made outdoors used reflectors ("the aid of mirrors") to keep the actors visible while sunshine opposite the camera gave the same edge-lighting effect to their bodies (Fig. 2.78) The shots employing a sunlight arc for selective illumination in night-for-night scenes would also have seemed novel to the Germans, as in a segment with a car on a road (Fig. 2.79). The very fact that the reviewer seems to think that even in interiors the back-lighting was created with "mirrors" suggests how unfamiliar the idea of putting lamps at the rear of the sets was in Germany.

The cinematographer of DADDY-LONG-LEGS and other Mary Pickford films was Charles Rosher, one of the great cameramen of the silent era and also one of the masters of back-lighting; he was to photograph Lubitsch's first Hollywood film, ROSITA. We could be almost certain just from circumstance that Lubitsch was influenced by DADDY-LONG-LEGS, but he also explicitly stated this to Robert Florey in an interview in 1923, during the filming of Rosita: "Earlier in Berlin I saw the old films of Mary Pickford [i.e., probably the Griffith Biographs], and more recently I particularly admired her artistry and her immense talent in Daddy Long Legs. I have endeavored, while shooting, to reconcile American methods and my own method of working, and I think that we will arrive at a good result."[16]

In 1921, Lubitsch had the chance to work in the American style when FP-L set up a new company in Berlin, called the Europäischen Film Allianz, or EFA. EFA leased an exhibition hall, originally built by furniture manufacturer Markiewicz and converted into a film studio in 1920 by Goron-Films.[17] It became the EFA-Atelier am Zoo, and EFA announced that it would equip it with the latest in filmmaking technology.[18] Several smaller German production firms were created to make films for EFA, including Ernst Lubitsch-Film. Thus Lubitsch's last two films made in Germany, Das Weib des Pharao and Die Flamme were American-financed.

The lighting style of the first film that Lubitsch made for EFA, Das Weib des Pharao, marked a radical change from his earlier German work. Suddenly we see a heavy dependence on back-lighting (Fig. 2.80). This shot also demonstrates how selective light could pick out parts of an impressive set without making it obtrusive and how edge light creates depth by making the character stand out against a relatively dark background. Another interior scene shows how bright light coming from the side makes the actors clearly visible without casting shadows onto the sets (Fig. 2.81). The side-light emphasizes the three-dimensionality of the large pillars but again prevents their unduly drawing the viewer's attention. A number of exteriors were shot at night, using large arc spotlights from the sides and rear (Fig. 2.82); in this and other scenes, flares (motivated as torches) supplement the arc light – a tactic Griffith had used five years earlier in the night battles in the Babylonian section of Intolerance. In Das Weib des Pharao, when a character is placed in darkness in the foreground, the effect is deliberate – caused by back-lighting rather than by the inevitable dark patch in the foreground of the V-lighting plot (Fig. 2.83). Here we see Lubitsch moving toward the mastery of lighting that he would gain in Hollywood; compare this shot with a similar silhouette effect in Rosita (Fig. 2.84).

Undoubtedly there are still many compositions which reflect the earlier German norms, as in one shot's unbalanced V-pattern light, casting conspicuous shadows on the set (Fig. 2.85). The film's most familiar image, however, showing the hero entering a ziggurat-style tomb, displays Lubitsch's understanding of how to apply the new equipment to which he has access (Fig. 2.86). A single sunlight arc placed at a steep angle above the set picks out the vertical "steps" in the ceiling and illuminates the hero, his arm casting a single, unobtrusive, and crisp shadow. A second sunlight arc at the top of the steps outlines him in light and creates another sharp-edged shadow of his figure almost un-noticeably on the floor where the bed nearly hides it. The surviving fragments from DIE FLAMME (1922) indicate a more modest production. The dark interiors that dominate these scenes contain American-style edge-lighting that subtly separates the actors from the sets (Figs. 2.87 and 2.88).

Few, if any, German filmmakers took to American-style lighting as quickly as Lubitsch did, and his transitional films seem to have been held up as models to be emulated. In May of 1922, a prominent Berlin film exporter returned from a tour of the US, declaring that the lighting equipment in the studios there was superior to that of the German facilities:

> Also the technique of lighting, using back-lighting and so forth to create images that appear to be stereoscopic, is much more advanced in America than in Germany. It is deplorable that the leading German firms, which put millions and millions into their film production, cannot finally decide to incur the one-time-only expense of modernizing their lighting installations and equipment. The fact that, with the help of a modern lighting installation one can achieve photography that meets American standards, is demonstrated by the most recent Lubitsch film, shot in the EFA studio.[19]

That film was DAS WEIB DES PHARAO, which had premiered two months earlier.

The same exporter had this to say about lighting and the prospects for selling German films in America:

> In part, our poor exchange rate can be blamed for the fact that few technical innovations in cameras and lamps have found their way into our studios, but it has certainly also been due to a great deal of laziness and myopia on the part of the large firms, and especially their production supervisors. Now, at last, one works with the unsurpassed Bell & Howell camera in Berlin; now finally one has access, at least in a few studios, to the new mercury-vapor lamps, the sunlight spotlights, and so on. Gradually directors and cameramen are now also working in the studio with back-lighting effects and no longer just shine a pair of lamps in from the right and left, as they did formerly, so that the image made the actors look stuck onto the set. Uncluttered, dark backgrounds, no overly furnished rooms, and effective back-lit photography are the main characteristics of technically good films.[20]

This was, in short, a description of the ideal Hollywood film. The phrase about actors looking "stuck onto the set" refers to the lack of back-lighting yielded by the V-pattern ("just shine a pair of lamps in from the right and left"). We have seen the results of placing dark hair and clothing against dark settings (Figs. 2.63 and 2.64).

Over the next few years, the technical changes called for were made. German firms built dark studios or darkened existing glass walls with paint or curtains, and they installed artificial-lighting systems. By the mid-1920s, many German films, at least those released by UFA, used a straightforward imitation of American lighting. The differences created by the war had been evened out. We shall examine the continuing German adoption of three-point lighting in Chapter 6.

Lubitsch Masters Three-point Lighting in Hollywood

By the time that Germany's technological updating was well under way, Lubitsch was already established in America. His films made there seldom contain generalized, diffuse lighting. Rather, selective lighting acts to differentiate areas within sets, to make the backgrounds visible but unobtrusive, to pull the actors forward in depth against the sets, to create dramatic compositions – in short, to contribute actively but subtly in the telling of the story in the classical manner.

A shot from THREE WOMEN offers a simple but powerful demonstration of Lubitsch's use of three-point lighting for dramatic purposes (Fig. 2.89). This is the establishing shot for a new scene, and its function is to convey immediately that the young woman at the table must eat alone because her irresponsible mother is away. The key light, in this case from above and motivated as coming from the hanging chandelier, not only picks out the daughter but also brightens the surface of the table, emphasizing how large it is for one person. The same point is made by the chairs, which have been pulled out from the table so that bright light can fall on their unoccupied cushions. The surrounding set, simple and elegant, needs simply to signify an upper-middle-class dining room, and it is visible in a subdued fill light.

More complicated scenes called for a combination of carefully aimed lamps. In this shot from ROSITA, for example, attention seems to have been given to the way light will strike every separate surface within this large, busy set (Fig. 2.90). Nearly invisible openings at the sides allow a great deal of light to be cast in, with fill eliminating most shadows yet giving a sense of depth through the highlights on the foreground arch, the table in the middle-ground, the sloping balustrade of the stairs at the rear, and on the arches beyond that. Lubitsch's developing skill at picking out different portions of a set with selective lighting also shapes the tavern scene early in FORBIDDEN PARADISE (Fig. 2.91). The most salient figure is the chauffeur at the center, who is picked out with a bright light against the dark wall at the rear. Strong back-lighting puts the faces of the couple at foreground left in semi-darkness, while the women at the left rear – one turned away from us – are clearly peripheral to the action.

Once Lubitsch discovered back-lighting, it became one of his main techniques. His actors are typically outlined with edge light, as in the interrogation scene of ROSITA (Fig. 2.92) or a simple two-shot conversation in THREE WOMEN (Fig. 2.93). A shot of Ronald Colman in the opening scene of LADY WINDERMERE'S FAN (Fig. 2.94) is probably as skillful a use of edge-lighting as one could find. Remarkably, the left sleeve, placed against the dark bookshelf at the rear, has a fairly broad highlight running along it, while the right one, backed by the lighter fireplace area, has a hair-thin outline. Each book on the shelf unobtrusively receives its own little highlight. By this point, Lubitsch has utterly assimilated the three-point system, and perhaps because he had come to it so late, he took the time to execute it just a bit better than anyone else. He also seems to have liked foreground silhouette effects. We have already seen one in ROSITA (Fig. 2.84). In FORBIDDEN PARADISE, Lubitsch creates a foreground and a background group of officers listening to a speaker on a table by lighting the rear plane brightly and placing the shadowed figures in the front against them (Fig. 2.95).

Most of these examples show Lubitsch minimizing shadows cast by the actors. Still, using bright arc lamps, he could ensure that deliberate, prominent shadows looked dark and crisp-edged, as in these examples from ROSITA (Fig. 2.96) and THREE WOMEN (Fig. 2.97). In Figure 2.96, one large spotlight from the right front picks out the columns and the woman's figure, creating a single deep shadow that allows her light dress to be seen against the similarly light wall behind her – essentially a reversal of back-light. The room beyond has been lit separately.

As we have already seen, Lubitsch used night-for-night shooting for DAS WEIB DES PHARAO, but the unmotivated spotlight on the sphinx (Fig. 2.82) and the flares reveal a director still feeling his way with this technique. ROSITA's carnival scene was shot at night, using large arc lamps and fireworks (Fig. 2.98). In FORBIDDEN PARADISE, a scene on a road at night uses discrete fill light on the foliage to create a backdrop to the action (Fig. 2.99). In one of the most charming moments of THE STUDENT PRINCE IN OLD HEIDELBERG, the two lovers search in vain for each other, then sit disconsolately on either side of a wall (Fig. 2.100). Lubitsch isolates each in a separate pool of light, darkening the top of the wall with plants and the shadows of leaves so that it will not appear as an eye-catching vertical shape; instead, our eye is guided outward toward the actors.

Lubitsch did not master three-point lighting instantly, and we can find some lingering examples of the dark zone in ROSITA, when the king exits to the side of the camera (Fig. 2.101 and Fig. 2.102). (It must be said that one can occasionally see this sort of dark-zone problems in the area just in front of the camera in Hollywood films, even into the sound era; they would, however, be considered mistakes for someone working within the classical system.) Perhaps as a result of Lubitsch's work with cinematographer Charles van Enger at Warner Bros., the characteristic unlit patch in the foreground disappears in the director's films after 1923.

As is evident from several of my examples here, an important goal of the three-point lighting system was to illuminate sets enough to be seen but not enough to draw the spectator's attention away from the actors. Similarly, parts of the set important to the action had to be singled out without the less significant areas receiving equal prominence, as Chapter 3 will show. Hollywood practitioners created a playing space that maximized the comprehensibility of the action using settings that worked along with lighting.

Three-point Lighting and Expressionism

The V-pattern of lighting may, in retrospect, seem to be a simple, old-fashioned approach that continued to be used after the War for want of a better one. It was eminently suited, however, to the most distinctively German style that arose after the War: German Expressionism. Expressionism depended on frequent graphic conjunctions between actor and set. When the film exporter quoted above complained about the V-pattern causing the actors to look "stuck on the sets," he was describing something that might be a problem for most filmmakers, but it was exactly what Expressionist designers wanted. Typically the Expressionist set had to be maximally visible to create the intended composition, and ideally the actor's three-dimensionality and separation from the set were minimized. Using three-point lighting in a scene like this one from GENUINE (Fig. 2.103) would make no sense. Indeed, there is little one can say about this lighting except that it is flat and even.

The adoption of three-point lighting in the German studios was well underway by 1924, the year in which one could say the Expressionist movement proper ended (with the long-delayed productions of FAUST, 1926 and METROPOLIS, 1927, providing a coda). Expressionist filmmakers were presumably free to ignore this stylistic change and continue to use flat frontal lighting. With each passing year, however, such films looked increasingly old-fashioned, and the glossy look and easy comprehensibility of more classical-style films clearly found more public acceptance. In lighting, I would argue that the American influence worked strongly against the continued use of the very techniques fundamental to the Expressionist film style.

3 Subduing the Cluttered Background: Set Design

Classical Norms of Set Design

The classical norms of Hollywood set design developed during the 1910s, parallel to the changes in lighting practice. Lighting and setting were closely linked, working together to create the overall pictorial identity of the scene as the actors moved about within a playing space. Key lights for actors and fill lights on sets maintained the proper balance, with the background visible but not distracting.

The set itself worked toward the same ideals. The set needed to be visible, for it gave the viewer salient information about the characters. But once that information had been absorbed, there was no point in having the settings conspicuously visible throughout a scene. In closer shots especially, settings needed to be noticeably present, but not really noticed. Critic Kenneth MacGowan summarized this notion beautifully in 1921 when he described the work of two American art directors. His first example is the rich interiors of Wilfred Buckland, who had worked with David Belasco on the stage and later with Cecil B. De Mille at Lasky. "Lasky Lighting," famous for its use of a single strong key with no fill or back light, had rendered his sets less visible in some films. MacGowan went on to describe the more recent, simpler sets designed Robert Brunton, who worked under contract to producer Thomas Ince:

> There was something else to the pictures of Lasky. There were backgrounds to catch the light into shadows. Because Buckland had worked with the master-realist of the stage, he brought something besides the Belasco plays to Lasky. He brought tasteful richness of setting. Under the flat lighting of most movies, it would have bored and distracted with quite the force that it did on the stage ... But made over by "Lasky Lighting" – as it is today in most Famous Players-Lasky productions – it has a splendid and satisfying richness.
>
> It is the danger of distracting the eyes from the actors by over-developing setting or costumes, which made the next contribution to the screen picture so immensely valuable. Another art director, Robert Brunton, under the supervision of Thomas H. Ince, understood that essential task in creative progress – elimination. He built his settings with taste and restraint, but he made assurance doubly sure by blotting them out with shadows. Realism and minutia he borrowed, and light from a single major source; but with one he killed the other. Through windows, doors, high casements or shaded lamps, he drove his light upon the actors of his films, and almost

upon the actors alone. They held the center of the stage, illumined and dramatized by light. Behind them were mere suggestions of place – surfaces that were at once atmosphere and a frame.[1]

As with lighting, the conception of ideal set design was quite different in Germany from that in the US. And as with lighting, Lubitsch made a rapid transition from one set of norms to the other.

As Janet Staiger noted in *The Classical Hollywood Cinema*, during the mid-1910s, Hollywood studios divided production tasks among greater numbers of specialists than their German counterparts. Before that time, set design had usually been handled by the stage manager, who was also in charge of the actual construction of the sets. It was around 1914 that we see the emergence of the position of art director.

Art directors were expected to create impressively beautiful or spectacularly large sets, and they were responsible for doing research to guarantee their historical and geographic accuracy. Some sets imitated the Italian epics, such as CABIRIA, that had recently enjoyed such an enormous vogue. During the mid- to late-1910s, Hollywood films often contained sets which attracted the eye, even when their appearances did not actively contribute to the drama. Their lavishness and authenticity often held an appeal distinct from that of the ongoing action. The Babylonian set in INTOLERANCE remains the most famous example, but there were others, such as Figure 3.1, which shows an interior scene from Lois Weber's THE DUMB GIRL OF PORTICI (1916). Such sets also tended to be distractingly prominent because they were usually lit by flat sunlight. Later Hollywood practice minimized this effect by constructing sets inside large dark studios lit by a variety of specially-constructed lamps. Germany and other European film-producing countries would follow that lead several years later.

By 1920 or so, a slightly modified conception of set design became apparent in Hollywood's discourse concerning its own practices. A set of guidelines was evolving, somewhat parallel to the continuity rules for editing. These guidelines would help make sets less obtrusive by largely subordinating their functions to the narrative action. Settings were still supposed to be historically accurate and to contribute to an attractive composition. They were also expected to establish the narrative situation by signaling the characteristics of their occupants quickly – especially their social stations. There evolved conventionalized upper-, middle-, and lower-class styles of domestic interiors. Thus the opening scene of William C. deMille's 1921 MISS LULU BETT quickly yet unobtrusively establishes a middle-class household as much by setting as by the action played out within it. After an establishing shot of a dining room, there are five closer shots of portions of the room (Fig. 3.2) before a return to the long shot for the first character's entrance.

Even while the sets were performing this establishing function, they were expected to be unobtrusive. (Most directors would certainly not have cut around within a set with no characters present, as deMille did.) The sets were meant to provide a sketchy rather than a cluttered background to the action in close shots. These ideals are apparent in various commentaries from the time. In 1921, one observer remarked on Gilbert White's sets for a Goldwyn film entitled THE HIGHEST BIDDER:

> In carrying out the mood of gentility and refinement as a background for the interplay of elemental passions, the settings add to the dramatic theme. Nor [sic] do they ever intrude to the weakening of the story. The characters move through the sets; we feel that they belong there; and, consequently, our attention is not distracted by speculations as to how such a room could belong to such a character.[2]

Here we find an expression of the classical Hollywood cinema's overall goal: to make all stylistic techniques serve the narrative by guiding the spectator's attention to the most dramatically salient aspects of the film, which are the characters and their actions. For this author, the sets "add to the dramatic theme" without obtruding. Hence "our attention is not distracted" by the sets.

Undoubtedly many sets of the mid- to late-1910s period, both outdoors and in the studio, continued to use lighting and busy design in such a way that the actors might not be picked out sufficiently against their surroundings. We can, however, see attempts to create less conspicuous settings. In the 1917 FIELD OF HONOR (Alan Holubar; Fig. 3.3), one set has a fairly busy pattern in the wallpaper (a trait we shall see frequently in German set design of the immediate post-War era). The filmmakers have muted the effect of the pattern by building the set against the sun, so that the brightest (key) light comes through the door (which frames the man entering) and window, while the walls receive ambient fill light. Another film from the same year, LOVE AND THE LAW (Fig. 3.4) contains a simple office set, with molding and curtains to indicate the back wall and window, and an uncluttered desk. The woman seated in the foreground left creates a sense of depth without the area between the camera and desk being obviously extended by the placement of furniture near the front of the playing space. In a somewhat higher-budget film made three years later, THE MARK OF ZORRO (1920, Fred Niblo; Fig. 3.5), a more elaborate but still relatively simple set frames the duel and onlookers. The arch on the doorway at the rear emphasizes the center, while the stairway at the left unobtrusively suggests the building around the characters. The floor contains small rugs to break up the stretch of flat space, but none of the patterns is noticeable enough to distract the eye.

These three examples are all box-style sets, with a back wall perpendicular or at only a slight angle to the camera's view. As we saw in the lighting chart in Figure 2.18, however, shooting obliquely along a long wall into an L-shaped set was common by the late 1910s. A long shot from HER CODE OF HONOR (1919, John C. Stahl; Fig. 3.6) fits this pattern, with enough furniture to suggest an upper-class sitting room without creating clutter, and with the background being darker than the foreground. As we shall see shortly, these various tactics to keep sets visible but unobtrusive were for the most part not used in German films of this period.

A major art director who helped establish the ideal of unobtrusive sets was Hugo Ballin. In 1921, he wrote: "Perfect sets have never made a drama. The audience follows story. The story can be explained by settings. Settings are dramatic rhetoric. They should be indicative of breeding. When settings receive uncommon notice the drama is defective."[3] This description echoes the universal assumption of Hollywood practitioners that story action proceeds continuously. The audience should not pause in following that ongoing action, even in order to linger over an attractive set or any other conspicuous stylistic flourish.

How to make settings unobtrusive? Partly through simplicity of design and partly through a use of selective lighting. Kenneth MacGowan described the simplifying of set design by Ballin at Goldwyn during 1919 and 1920:

> He has left unornamented the solid walls that beaverboard allowed the studios to substitute for the canvas of the stage. He has used draperies ingeniously, constructing a Sherry's handsomer than Sherry's out of a few tall stone pillars and some heavy curtains. He has applied design skillfully and with discretion. Above all he has kept his backgrounds subdued and his floor free of cluttering furniture. Consequently, the actors can be easily detected on the screen, even by the most unpracticed eye.[4]

The suggestion here is that the sets would be dressed in a manner simpler than might be strictly realistic. For Hollywood practitioners, however, realism was ultimately less important than narrative clarity. MacGowan's mention of draperies gives a further clue to Hollywood set construction during the 1920s. Large drapes formed walls, divided sets, suggested windows or doors, and framed whole settings. Although draperies were not a significant factor in Lubitsch's German sets, we shall see them used prominently in his American films.

In 1921, one ideal of Hollywood set design and photography was established by Rex Ingram's enormously popular film, THE FOUR HORSEMEN OF THE APOCALYPSE. It was shot by one of the master cinematographers of the silent period, John Seitz. The introduction of the hero (Rudolph Valentino in his star-making role) took place in an Argentinian tango hall, with a strong composi-

tion created by a dark arch in the foreground and the main characters silhou-
etted against a background softened by smoke (Fig. 3.7). Closer shots in the
subsequent conversation scene in this same set make the setting hazy and the
characters distinct (Fig. 3.8). Both the set design and Seitz's cinematography in
these scenes were directly imitated by Lubitsch in some of his Hollywood
films.

Lubitsch and German Set Design

The sorts of changes in Hollywood practice that I have been describing were
not paralleled in Germany, or indeed in any other European film-producing
countries in general. In Germany, attractive sets, whether they were used for
epics or ordinary locales, remained the ideal. Set designers often got more
prominent billing and proportionately higher pay than their American counterparts. Even a survey of relatively ordinary German films from the period
1918 to 1922 reveals many eye-catching sets that were either elegantly designed, had extreme depth (requiring long walks by actors before they came
into close camera range), cluttered set dressing, or a combination of all of these
elements.

Undoubtedly the German cinema of this period contains many lovely sets,
such as this large but simple set in Die Ehe der Fürstin Demidoff (Fig. 3.9).
Used less adeptly, however, the deep space of such sets could look old-fashioned. In Hollywood, creating a back wall and then making the playing space
look larger often involved placing chairs or other furniture near the camera – a
practice that began around 1910 and largely disappeared by the end of World
War I. The Germans continued to use it for a few more years. Mr. Wu, which
appears to have been a fairly high-budget film for 1918, has a number of beautiful but busy sets (Fig. 3.10). Not only do the upper parts of the walls have eye-
catching decoration, but the placement of the centered rear doorway and the
foreground desk near the camera made the entering actor appear somewhat
overwhelmed by his surroundings until he moves forward. Less skillfully designed sets could look strangely disproportional, as in this sitting-room set
from Marionetten des Teufels (Fig. 3.11). The three steps more-or-less at the
center in the rear mark the main entrance to the set, leaving actors a bit of a
hike to reach the foreground playing area. A sparsely furnished set, like the office from Die Trommeln Asiens (Fig. 3.12), could make the broad gap between entrance and foreground look strange indeed.

Elaborate combinations of furniture, bric-a-brac, and above all, densely
patterned wallpaper create cluttered compositions in many films of the era.

Figure 3.13 shows a bedroom and sitting room in DIE EHE DER FÜRSTIN DEMIDOFF (1921). The busy wallpaper, the elaborate columns, a rococo bed, the centrally placed painting, the combination of three rooms, and the prominent, striped sofa all combine to overwhelm the action. One actor by the arched doorway at the right is inconspicuous by comparison, and a second player, difficult to see even when moving, occupies the bed in the room at the rear. In particular, highly patterned wallpaper continued to be common in German films in this era. In I.N.R.I. (Fig. 3.14), wallpaper, rug, and furniture combine to create a more middle-class, but still cluttered bedroom. Such settings were more obviously distracting in long shots, as is the case in another large set from MARIONETTEN DES TEUFELS (Fig. 3.15), but closer framings keep the patterned wallpaper conspicuous because of the overall diffused sunlight (Fig. 3.16). In Figure 3.17, from DIE LIEBSCHAFTEN DES HEKTOR DALMORE (1921), the protagonist's apartment is a deep space with walls zigzagging at odd angles, hung with paintings that glaringly reflect the flat frontal light; a patterned carpet and heaps of cushions add to the complicated arrangement. Indeed, another part of this apartment contains the same striped sofa (Fig. 3.18) we have just seen in DIE EHE DER FÜRSTIN DEMIDOFF (Fig. 3.13), and I have spotted it in a third film of the period as well. Its striking shape and contrasting colors clearly made it an exemplary set element by German standards. By American standards, however, these and many other German sets of this period look old-fashioned, reminiscent of early to mid-1910s filmmaking.

One remarkable interview with Lubitsch from 1916 suggests that the young director and star had ideas about set design that were not all that different from those developing in Hollywood at the same time:

> He is of the view that the scenery must be first-class – that is, beautiful and full of style. But the scenery designs must not predominate, must not, as we so often see, become the main thing. He means that the effort to place huge sets and vast expanses in the image affects the placement of the camera, and as a result the acting of the players will be overlooked. This acting, however, always remains the truly central element, the fiber of the whole thing. For that reason, every important shot should be taken solely and entirely with medium-long shots. In that way the finest nuances of the changing expressions also achieve their full value.[5]

This opinion now seems ironic, since Lubitsch was soon to become famous internationally for the beautiful, amusing, or spectacular sets in his films. Still, it shows that he would have been receptive to classical norms when given a chance to work in Hollywood.

Indeed, in his German films, Lubitsch's approach to sets sticks pretty closely to the norms of his country's cinema. There were two major differences. First, due to his immediate success as a director of features, his films often had higher budgets than those of most of his contemporaries. Second, he worked with prominent and skilled designers. Hence his German sets, primarily designed by Kurt Richter and, less frequently, Ernst Stern (a prominent designer for Max Reinhardt), are often more skillfully done than usual, and their visual traits assume an unusually prominent role in the creation of the action. Precisely because they are frequently beautiful or clever in their own right, they often draw the eye away from the actors. In this sense, Lubitsch and other German filmmakers working in the same vein were following the model of hugely successful pre-World War I Italian epics, such as CABIRIA.

Sets are particularly prominent in Lubitsch's stylized comedies such as DIE AUSTERNPRINZESSIN, where he calls attention to the elaborate figure on the floor by having the actor pace out its pattern in several shots (Fig. 3.19). This comic device has drawn much attention.[6] Lubitsch himself has commented on it:

> I remember a piece of business which caused a lot of comment at the time. A poor man had to wait in the magnificent entrance hall of the home of a multi-millionaire. The parquet floor of the multi-millionaire's home was of a most complicated design. The poor man in order to overcome his impatience and his humiliation after waiting for hours walked along the outlines of the very intricate pattern on the floor. It is very difficult to describe this nuance, and I don't know if I succeeded, but it was the first time I turned from comedy to satire.[7]

Lubitsch tended to use settings with this kind of rosette pattern, as in this later scene from the eunuchs' quarters in the 1920 Arabian-Nights fantasy, SUMURUN (Fig. 3.20). In one of the most interesting studies of Lubitsch, Eithne and Jean-Loup Bourget argue that rosette-patterned floors are part of the Viennese Secessionist style in Lubitsch's films and are used in a comic-operetta manner to connote luxury and wealth.[8] Lancelot's approach to Hilarius's doll shop in DIE PUPPE provides an instance of a similar kind of set that draws the eye of the spectator away from the actor in a less obvious way (Fig. 3.21). In terms of the logic of the story, the elaborate pillars and painted figures are not necessary. This building has already been established as a doll shop. A similar dispersion of attention occurs again inside the shop, as the cluttered interior creates a humor of its own – one that is incidental to the narrative line. It is also the kind of humor that Hollywood seldom used.[9] By the way, one seldom sees evidence of Lubitsch's direct influence on his German contemporaries, but one set from DIE NACHT DER EINBRECHER (Fig. 3.22) seems likely to be modeled on those in Lubitsch's comedies, especially DIE AUSTERNPRINZESSIN.

Lubitsch's historical films use sets in a way that is more familiar from pre-World War I Italian epics and Hollywood films from the mid-1910s, drawing the eye because of their considerable size and elaborate lines. The pattern was

established in a modest way in Lubitsch's second feature, CARMEN, in 1918 –
though even here the budget was probably higher than that of most German
films. Here the town square (Fig. 3.23), with its alternation of lower buildings
with higher, tower-like upper stories, was typical of the main sets Richter created for Lubitsch (here, as in most of his German films, built on the backlot at
Union's Tempelhof studio). Historian Jan-Christopher Horak has commented
that "[t]he hot, sun-baked streets and Spanish style white houses of Lubitsch's
Seville looked credible because of their careful design and three-
dimensionality which was reinforced by Lubitsch having his actors play in
and around the sets, rather than in front of them."[10] These buildings were
framework structures finished on only two or three sides, but they could be
photographed from several angles to create a sense of figures moving through
a large space. American studios were using similar façades for costume pictures and epics, as in Griffith's ORPHANS OF THE STORM (1922; Fig. 3.24).

A year later, in 1919, Lubitsch made the epic that established his reputation
outside Germany, MADAME DUBARRY. The film was a substantial hit in New
York in late 1920 and early 1921, largely on the basis of its spectacular sets and
crowd scenes and its star, Pola Negri. It was widely estimated that while the
film had been made for the equivalent of approximately $40,000 in Germany, it
would have cost about $500,000 to replicate in Hollywood – still a substantial
budget in a town that had yet to see its first million-dollar film (which came,
according to Universal's publicity, with Erich von Stroheim's FOOLISH WIVES,
1922).

What the American commentators could not have known is that one of the
most impressive sets in MADAME DUBARRY was recycled from CARMEN. Compare Figure 3.25, the main city square in which the French revolutionaries riot,
with Figure 3.23. The four-pillared building at the left was reused with a
slightly different roof, and the buildings at the rear center and right were
adapted, expanded versions of the tower-like structures I remarked upon earlier. Thus the similarities of Richter's sets for the historical films as a group involve more than just his decorative style. It seems likely that the same core set
elements were left standing and served as the starting point for several of these
films. Sets were recycled in this way in Hollywood as well (as when the MAG-
NIFICENT AMBERSONS stairway reappeared in Val Lewton films), but these
subsequent re-uses tended to be in cheaper films. Lubitsch managed to up-
grade his films as he reused his sets. Once he got to Hollywood, the sets for his
films were designed and built from the ground up.

Apart from the studio back-lot sets, for MADAME DUBARRY Lubitsch was
able to shoot the exterior scenes at the palace of Sans Souci in Potsdam, which
stood in for Versailles (Fig. 3.26). This was the sort of spectacular European period building that had no real equivalent in the US.

In almost every country where it showed, MADAME DUBARRY won enthusiastic praise for its sets. One dissenting view came from Hollywood, however in the form of a letter published in German in the summer 1921 issue of *Die Kinotechnik*, then Germany's leading technical film publication. The letter was signed by one C.A.L., credited as a prominent technical expert working in Hollywood. (The author was most likely Chester A. Lyons, who had for some years been a regular cinematographer working for producer Thomas H. Ince and who, in 1921, became Frank Borzage's regular cameraman.) He lauded certain aspects of the film, such as its performances and the excellent Agfa film stock. C.A.L. was, however, less kind concerning the sets: "Some of the sets are pathetic! They look as if the film had been shot 10-15 years ago." He singles out a scene near the end when a disguised Armand Defoux enters a prison cell in order to save DuBarry:

> One can discern each brushstroke on the sheets of plywood. How can one produce the effect of that kind of stone wall by using roofing material with the cracks smeared with tar? The scenery of the cellar tavern in which Dubarry fetches her drunken brother frankly smells of fresh lumber. If we [i.e., Hollywood filmmakers] require the effect of old, messy walls, then we paint the pine sheet that we use for them a medium brown, first throwing a handful of sawdust in the paint. This paint then dries so that the surface looks cracked, rough, and old.[11]

A look at the scene in question (Fig. 3.27) shows that the "stone walls" behind the actors are quite evidently painted flats, an effect made all the more apparent by the frontal flood lighting. It seems almost certain that Lubitsch read C.A.L.'s letter, and it must have carried an unaccustomed sting amid the nearly universal praise for the film. As we shall see, Lubitsch soon abandoned this kind of obviously painted settings.

Through most of his German career, Lubitsch stuck to the German norm of building interior sets in the open air, lit by undiffused sunlight. His first dramatic feature, DIE AUGEN DER MUMIE MÂ has a typical interior of this sort (Fig. 3.28). The huge set representing the auditorium at the Opera in MADAME DUBARRY is similarly open to direct sunlight (Fig. 3.29). The huge cathedral in ANNA BOLEYN (Fig. 2.52) represents an interior space. These sets somewhat resemble the spectacular ones in INTOLERANCE and THE DUMB GIRL OF PORTICI (Fig. 3.1). Yet in Hollywood practice, the idea of building a large interior set outdoors and filming it in stark daylight was considered outmoded by 1920.

Another Lubitsch scene that exemplifies how decor was conspicuously displayed occurs early in MADAME DUBARRY. The heroine waits to be admitted to dine with a rich admirer. A curtain is suddenly drawn aside by an invisible hand to reveal the first of many rich interiors (Figs. 3.30 and 3.31).[12] In such scenes, we may conclude that the set designs overrun their narrative functions in ways that Hollywood practice would by this point tend to discourage. Still, spectacle continued to be valued in American filmmaking, as long as a strong narrative motivated its use. The ORPHANS OF THE STORM (1922) street set mentioned above provides an example (Fig. 3.24). Surely, however, spectators' eyes do not linger on the set. Rather, they are fastened on the drama of the two separated orphans – the blind one on a balcony and her sister passing in the street – nearly finding each other. Such a commitment to spectacle within Hollywood filmmaking may help explain why Lubitsch's historical films were imported to the US, while his comedies were not.[13]

Lubitsch continued to use visually prominent sets until nearly the end of his German career. DIE BERGKATZE takes the stylization of the earlier comedies to even greater extremes, framing many of Ernst Stern's flamboyant designs with variously shaped masks (Fig. 3.32).

Lubitsch's last two German features were financed by Paramount through its short-lived Berlin production subsidiary, the Europäischen Film-Allianz (EFA). Although EFA's large, American-style studio altered Lubitsch's lighting style noticeably, the sets for DAS WEIB DES PHARAO were, judging from the forty-some minutes of the original film that survive, largely in the old German epic style. Again Ernst Stern did the designs. As an amateur Egyptologist, he was in a position to render the sets, statues, and even some of the hieroglyphic texts with a semblance of authenticity.[14] Moreover, Paramount's backing meant that the film budget ran to $75,000, almost twice what American experts had estimated that MADAME DUBARRY cost. In his autobiography, Stern recalled that all of the sets were built full-sized, with no use of miniatures: "There was no difficulty about finance, as we were working for American backers. It was still the inflation period, and even a single dollar was quite a lot of money, so we had no time-robbing financial calculations to make, and we went to work cheerfully with a 'Damn the expense' attitude." For earlier films, Lubitsch's large sets had been built on the backlot at Union's Tempelhof studio, but the sets for WEIB were constructed on a leased open stretch of land in Steglitz, a Berlin suburb; the site was surrounded by modern buildings, and the sets had to be tall enough to block the view of these.[15] Now there could be no refitting of standing sets like the old town-square from CARMEN, MADAME DUBARRY, and perhaps other Lubitsch epics. Stern's sets (Fig. 3.33) prefigure those in Cecil B. DeMille's THE TEN COMMANDMENTS, made for Paramount about a year later (Fig. 3.34). We have already seen how Lubitsch used selective lighting for interior settings for this film, as well as for nighttime exteriors (Figs. 2.80 to 2.83, 2.86).

The scenes surviving from Lubitsch's last German film, DIE FLAMME, are filmed primarily in close framings with considerable editing in shot/reverse-shot patterns. Lighting tends to pick out the actors and downplay the settings.

Even in a medium-long framing that serves as a re-establishing shot (Fig. 3.35), the setting is not nearly as eye-catching as in Lubitsch's earlier films. It is difficult to draw conclusions on the basis of these fragments, but it may well be that Lubitsch was drawing close to the Hollywood ideal in his last German film.

Herr Lubitsch Goes to Hollywood

Lubitsch's first film in the States, ROSITA, was an historical film and resembled his German work in some ways. The large set representing Rosita's family's humble home overwhelms the human figures, with the archway in the foreground creating a distinctive composition (Fig. 2.90). The exteriors were familiar Lubitsch-style town squares with tower-like buildings – in this case created using glass shots for the upper elements of the set Fig. 3.36). The biggest set built for ROSITA was the enormous prison courtyard, with its looming gallows (Fig. 3.37). This set appears in several scenes, sometimes lit simply by the sun, but in night scenes like this one, lit selectively with large arc lamps. A large cathedral set (Fig. 3.38) provides an interesting contrast with the one in ANNA BOLEYN (Fig. 2.52). Here only the lower portion of the building has been built, with a glass shot supplying the ceiling and the upper parts of the walls. The join between the real and painted set elements is quite apparent: while the bottom portion is lit with diffused sunlight, the glass-shot artist has carefully painted key and fill light into the upper reaches of the cathedral.

For a smaller scene that takes places in a prison cell, Lubitsch proved that, with the help of set designer Svend Gade,[16] he could create a more acceptably realistic set than the one in MADAME DUBARRY that had attracted C.A.L.'s adverse comments (Fig. 3.39). Robert Florey, who was an assistant to Pickford and Fairbanks during this period and who watched the first few days of shooting on ROSITA, commented simply, "The first scene of ROSITA was shot in a set representing a sordid Spanish prison. Built in one of the 'east' corners of the covered studio, this set was small, but it did not have the feeling of a set, and that is all that was required of it."[17] Lubitsch was conforming to Hollywood's norms of lighting and set design.

Unlike Lubitsch's thrifty practice of rebuilding sets in Germany, the large sets for ROSITA were not reshaped for future productions – by Lubitsch or any one else. They were built on the same large backlot used for the ROBIN HOOD castle and other United Artists pictures by Fairbanks. The day after shooting on ROSITA ended on May 31, 1922, destruction of the ROSITA sets began in order to make room for THE THIEF OF BAGDAD (1924) sets.[18]

After his move to Warner Bros., Lubitsch abruptly abandoned his Germanic-style sets for the full-blown Hollywood approach. (He would, however, revive the German approach somewhat for his next film, FORBIDDEN PARADISE.) It was not simply a matter of changing genres from a large historical film to modern comedies. The sets in the Warner Bros. films also differ markedly from those in Lubitsch's German comedies. The sets for THE MARRIAGE CIRCLE were designed by a team who worked regularly at that studio: Lewis Geib and Esdras Hartley. The pair had already developed a fairly conventional approach, using mostly blank, paneled walls, a few pieces of furniture, and a ceiling lamp or chandelier hanging in the upper center of the frame. Small wall lamps and a few paintings or mirrors completed the simple, economical sets appropriate to a low-budget studio.

When working for Lubitsch, Geib and Harley had bigger budgets than usual at their disposal. Still, they created some fairly conventional sets unobtrusively to convey the well-to-do, upper-middle-class environment of the characters, as in the Brauns' drawing room, with its tall gray walls and single painting, its discreet shelves, its chandelier, its piano in the foreground left balanced against the door at the right (Fig. 3.40). The *Film Daily*'s reviewer praised Lubitsch's direction in general and commented specifically on "the lack of heavy backgrounds."[19]

Although Lubitsch treated most of the settings in this film with a similar conventional simplicity, he went further in one case. The *New York Times* reviewer noted with remarkable acumen that one set had been simplified beyond the bounds of realism: "Lubitsch reduced furnishings to the barest necessities, believing that too much furniture detracts attention from the players. Frequently in this picture he shows a medium shot with one of the characters posed against an empanelled door for a background."[20] And indeed, the door of Prof. Braun and Mizzi's bedroom is, unlike other doors in the film, quite blank, permitting Adolf Menjou to play two virtuoso passages before it (in medium shot) without the set distracting our attention in the least (Fig. 3.41); I shall analyze one of these in detail in Chapter Five. Many commentators have remarked on Lubitsch's use of doors as active elements in the dramatic content of scenes – either as frames for the players or in a series to move them among spaces.[21] THE MARRIAGE CIRCLE is perhaps the first film where Lubitsch used doors systematically, though a number of dramatic scenes are played in doorways in ANNA BOLEYN.

For his second Warner Bros. film, THREE WOMEN, Lubitsch turned to a more melodramatic subject matter and collaborated again with his ROSITA designer, Svend Gade. The film survives in a somewhat truncated form, but it is clear that a considerable budget allowed Lubitsch to integrate contemporary settings. The early charity ball set was designed on an enormous scale (and was

Chapter 1 Lubitsch's Career

Fig. 1.1 – Lubitsch (with megaphone) and the cameras used on Das Weib des Pharao, including two American Bell & Howells, second and third cameras from the left

Chapter 2 Lighting

Fig. 2.1 – Interior of the American Biograph studio in New York in 1909

Fig. 2.2 – A six-unit mercury-vapor lighting unit on a floor stand

Fig. 2.3 – Another six-unit mercury-vapor unit equipped to be hung above a set

Fig. 2.4 – Various types of American arc lamps

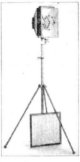

Fig. 2.5 – A double-carbon arc unit manufactured Germany

Fig. 2.6 – A Weinert hanging arc lamp

Fig. 2.7 – John Collins directing The Children of E

Fig. 2.8 – Arc floodlights on a multiple-unit stand

Fig. 2.9 – Interior of the JOFA-Atelier

Fig. 2.10 – Kliegl arc spotlights

Fig. 2.11 – A German-made arc spotlight

Fig. 2.12 – An American Sunlight arc lamp with its accessories

Fig. 2.13 – Using a Sunlight arc during exterior shooting

Fig. 2.14 – A German-made high-intensity arc lamp

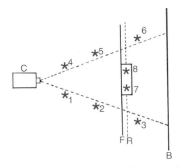

Fig. 2.15 – A 1921 German lighting plot

Fig. 2.16 – The exterior of the Union studio

Fig. 2.17 – The interior of the Union studio

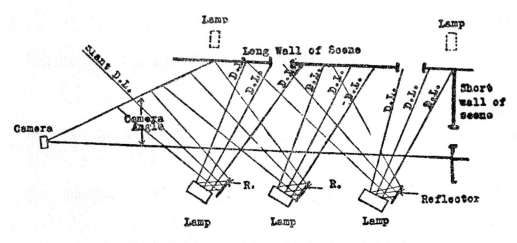

Fig. 2.18 – A 1919 American lighting plot showing an L-shaped set

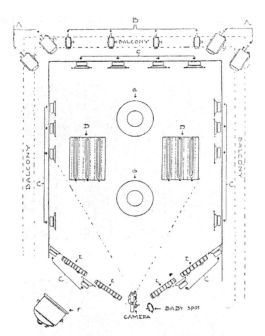

Fig. 2.19 – A 1923 American lighting plot for a box
set

Fig. 2.20 – The Famous Players-Lasky studio in 19

Fig. 2.21 – Lighting arrangement for a set in a dar
studio (c. 1925).

Fig. 2.22 – Multi-directional lighting in Robin Hood

Fig. 9.—Spotlighting is used in this set to separate the characters from the background and to accentuate the predominating features.

Fig. 10 —The value and necessity of highlights are appreciated when this illustration is compared with Figure 9.

Fig. 2.23 – A comparison demonstrating the benfits of backlighting

Fig. 2.24 – The Ghost of Rosie Taylor

Fig. 2.25 – The Ghost of Rosie Taylor

Fig. 2.26 – Mr. Wu

Fig. 2.27 – Die Brüder Karamassoff

Fig. 2.28 – Die Puppe

Fig. 2.29 – Kohlhiesels Töchter

Fig. 2.30 – Lubitsch (in vest) directing Sumurun

Fig. 2.31 – Sumurun

Fig. 2.32 – Mr. Wu

Fig. 2.33 – Landstrasse und Grossstadt

Fig. 2.34 – Carmen

Fig. 2.36 – Madame Dubarry

Fig. 2.37 – Rose Bernd

Fig. 2.38 – Sumurun

Fig. 2.39 – Anna Boleyn

Fig. 2.40 – Die Liebschaften des Hektor Dalmore

Fig. 2.41 – Carmen

Fig. 2.42 – Die Ehe der Fürstin Demidoff

Fig. 2.43 – Die Brüder Karamassof

Fig. 2.44 – Mr. Wu

Fig. 2.45 – Die weisse Pfau

Fig. 2.46 – Madame Dubarry

Fig. 2.47 – Die Augen der Mumie Mâ

Fig. 2.48 – Madame Dubarry

Fig. 2.49 – Madame Dubarry

Fig. 2.50 – I.N.R.I.: Die Katastrophe eines Volkes

Fig. 2.51 – Der weisse Pfau

Fig. 2.52 – Anna Boleyn

Fig. 2.53 – Rose Bernd

Fig. 2.54 – Der weisse Pfau

Fig. 2.55 – Kohlhiesels Töchter

Fig. 2.56 – Nerven

Fig. 2.57 – Die Ehe der Fűrstin Demidoff

Fig. 2.58 – Romeo und Julia im Schnee

Fig. 2.59 – Die Bergkatze

Fig. 2.60 – Rose Bernd

Fig. 2.61 – Carmen

Fig. 2.62 – Die Augen der Mumie Mâ

Fig. 2.63 – Meyer aus Berlin

Fig. 2.64 – Romeo und Julia im Schnee

Fig. 2.65 – Rose Bernd

Fig. 2.66 – Landstrasse und Grossstadt

Fig. 2.67 – Die Puppe

Fig. 2.68 – Madame Dubarry

Fig. 2.69 – Mr. Wu

Fig. 2.70 – Die Liebschaften des Hektor Dalmore

Fig. 2.71 – Die Liebschaften des Hektor Dalmore

Fig. 2.72 – Madame Dubarry

Fig. 2.73 – Madame Dubarry

Fig. 2.74 – Madame Dubarry

Fig. 2.75 – Die Austernprinzessin

Fig. 2.76 – Die Austernprinzessin

Fig. 2.77 – Daddy-Long-Legs

Fig. 2.78 – Daddy-Long-Legs

Fig. 2.79 – Daddy-Long-Legs

Fig. 2.80 – Das Weib des Pharao

Fig. 2.81 – Das Weib des Pharao

Fig. 2.82 – Das Weib des Pharao

Fig. 2.83 – Das Weib des Pharao

Fig. 2.84 – Rosita

Fig. 2.85 – Das Weib des Pharao

Fig. 2.86 – Das Weib des Pharao

Fig. 2.87 – Die Flamme

Fig. 2.88 – Die Flamme

Fig. 2.89 – Three Women

Fig. 2.90 – Rosita

Fig. 2.91 – Forbidden Paradise

Fig. 2.92 – Rosita

Fig. 2.93 – Three Women

Fig. 2.94 – Lady Windermere's Fan

Fig. 2.95 – Forbidden Paradise

Fig. 2.96 – Rosita

Fig. 2.97 – Three Women

Fig. 2.98 – Rosita

Fig. 2.99 – Forbidden Paradise

Fig. 2.100 – The Student Prince in Old Heidelberg

Fig. 2.101 – Rosita

Fig. 2.102 – Rosita

Fig. 2.103 – Genuine

Chapter 3 Set Design

Fig. 3.1 – The Dumb Girl of Portici

Fig. 3.2 – Miss Lulu Bett

Fig. 3.3 – Field of Honor

Fig. 3.4 – Love and the Law

Fig. 3.5 – The Mask of Zorro

Fig. 3.6 – Her Code of Honor

Fig. 3.7 – The Four Horsemen of the Apocalypse

Fig. 3.8 – The Four Horsemen of the Apocalypse

Fig. 3.9 – Die Ehe der Furstin Demidoff

Fig. 3.10 – Mr. Wu

Fig. 3.11 – Marionetten des Teufels

Fig. 3.12 – Die Trommeln Asians

Fig. 3.13 – Die Ehe der Fürstin Demidoff

Fig. 3.14 – I.N.R.I.: Die Katastrophe eines Volkes

Fig. 3.15 – Marionetten des Teufels

Fig. 3.16 – Marionetten des Teufels

Fig. 3.17 – Die Liebschaften der Hektor Dalmore

Fig. 3.18 – Die Liebschaften der Hektor Dalmore

Fig. 3.19 – Die Austernprinzessin

Fig. 3.20 – Sumurun

Fig. 3.21 – Die Puppe

Fig. 3.22 – Die Nacht der Einbrecher

Fig. 3.23 – Carmen

Fig. 3.24 – Orphans of the Storm

Fig. 3.25 – Madame Dubarry

Fig. 3.26 – Madame Dubarry

Fig. 3.27 – Madame Dubarry

Fig. 3.28 – Die Augen der Mumie Mâ

Fig. 3.29 – Madame Dubarry

Fig. 3.30 – Madame Dubarry

Fig. 3.31 – Madame Dubarry

Fig. 3.32 – Die Bergkatze

Fig. 3.33 – Das Weib des Pharao

Fig. 3.34 – The Ten Commandments

Fig. 3.35 – Die Flamme

Fig. 3.36 – Rosita

Fig. 3.37 – Rosita

Fig. 3.38 – Rosita

Fig. 3.39 – Rosita

Fig. 3.40 – The Marriage Circle

Fig. 3.41 – The Marriage Circle

Fig. 3.42 – Three Women

Fig. 3.43 – Three Women

Fig. 3.44 – Three Women

Fig. 3.45 – Forbidden Paradise

Fig. 3.46 – Lady Windermere's Fan

Fig. 3.47 – Lady Windermere's Fan

Fig. 3.48 – Lady Windermere's Fan

Fig. 3.49 – So This Is Paris

Fig. 3.50 – So This Is Paris

Fig. 3.51 – The Student Prince in Old Heidelberg

Fig. 3.52 – The Student Prince in Old Heidelbe

Chapter 4　Editing

Fig. 4.1 – Lubitsch editing Die Flamme

Fig. 4.2 – Mr. Wu

Fig. 4.3 – Mr. Wu

Fig. 4.4 – Mr. Wu

Fig. 4.5 – Mr. Wu

Fig. 4.6 – Die weisse Pfau

Fig. 4.7 – Die weisse Pfau

Fig. 4.8 – Die Ehe der Fürstin Demidoff

Fig. 4.9 – Die Ehe der Fürstin Demidoff

Fig. 4.10 – Rose Bernd

Fig. 4.11 – Rose Bernd

Fig. 4.12 – Ich möchte kein Mann sein!

Fig. 4.13 – Ich möchte kein Mann sein!

Fig. 4.14 – Sumurun

Fig. 4.15 – Sumurun

Fig. 4.16 – Sumurun

Fig. 4.17 – Sumurun

Fig. 4.18 – Sumurun

Fig. 4.19 – Carmen

Fig. 4.20 – Carmen

Fig. 4.21 – Die Brüder Karamassoff

Fig. 4.22 – Die Brüder Karamassoff

Fig. 4.23 – Die Bergkatze

Fig. 4.24 – Die Bergkatze

Fig. 4.25 – Landstrasse und Grossstadt

Fig. 4.26 – Landstrasse und Grossstadt

Fig. 4.27 – Landstrasse und Grossstadt

Fig. 4.28 – Landstrasse und Grossstadt

Fig. 4.29 – Landstrasse und Grossstadt

Fig. 4.30 – Landstrasse und Grossstadt

Fig. 4.31 – Landstrasse und Grossstadt

Fig. 4.32 – Die weisse Pfau

Fig. 4.33 – Die weisse Pfau

Fig. 4.34 – Die weisse Pfau

Fig. 4.35 – Die weisse Pfau

Fig. 4.36 – Die weisse Pfau

Fig. 4.37 – Die weisse Pfau

Fig. 4.38 – Die Augen der Mumie Mâ

Fig. 4.39 – Die Augen der Mumie Mâ

Fig. 4.40 – Die Augen der Mumie Mâ

Fig. 4.41 – Die Augen der Mumie Mâ

Fig. 4.42 – Die Augen der Mumie Mâ

Fig. 4.43 – Die Augen der Mumie Mâ

Fig. 4.44 – Die Augen der Mumie Mâ

Fig. 4.45 – Die Augen der Mumie Mâ

Fig. 4.46 – Die Augen der Mumie Mâ

Fig. 4.47 – Die Augen der Mumie Mâ

Fig. 4.48 – Madame Dubarry

Fig. 4.49 – Madame Dubarry

Fig. 4.50 – Madame Dubarry

Fig. 4.51 – Madame Dubarry

Fig. 4.52 – Madame Dubarry

Fig. 4.53 – Madame Dubarry

Fig. 4.54 – Madame Dubarry

Fig. 4.55 – Die Brüder Karamassoff

Fig. 4.56 – Die Brüder Karamassoff

Fig. 4.57 – Die Brüder Karamassoff

Fig. 4.58 – Die Liebschaften des Hektor Dalmore

Fig. 4.59 – Die Liebschaften des Hektor Dalmore

g. 4.60 – Die Liebschaften des Hektor Dalmore

Fig. 4.61 – Die Liebschaften des Hektor Dalmore

g. 4.62 – Die Liebschaften des Hektor Dalmore

Fig. 4.63 – Die Liebschaften des Hektor Dalmore

g. 4.64 – Die Liebschaften des Hektor Dalmore

Fig. 4.65 – Die Liebschaften des Hektor Dalmore

g. 4.66 – Die Liebschaften des Hektor Dalmore

Fig. 4.67 – Romeo und Julia im Schnee

Fig. 4.68 – Romeo und Julia im Schnee

Fig. 4.69 – Anna Boleyn

Fig. 4.70 – Anna Boleyn

Fig. 4.71 – Sumurun

Fig. 4.72 – Sumurun

Fig. 4.73 – Sumurun

Fig. 4.74 – Sumurun

Fig. 4.75 – Sumurun

Fig. 4.76 – Sumurun

Fig. 4.77 – Sumurun

Fig. 4.78 – Carmen

Fig. 4.79 – Carmen

Fig. 4.80 – Carmen

Fig. 4.81 – Carmen

Fig. 4.82 – Carmen

Fig. 4.83 – Carmen

Fig. 4.84 – Carmen

Fig. 4.85 – Carmen

Fig. 4.86 – Carmen

Fig. 4.87 – Carmen

Fig. 4.88 – Die Puppe

Fig. 4.89 – Die Puppe

Fig. 4.90 – Die Puppe

Fig. 4.91 – Die Puppe

Fig. 4.92 – Die Puppe

Fig. 4.93 – Sumurun

Fig. 4.94 – Sumurun

Fig. 4.95 – Sumurun

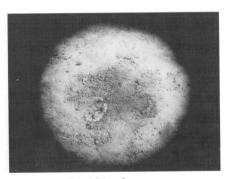

Fig. 4.96 – Sumurun

Fig. 4.97 – Sumurun

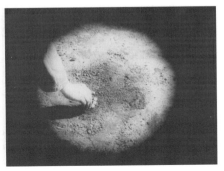

Fig. 4.98 – Sumurun

Fig. 4.99 – Sumurun

Fig. 4.100 – Sumurun

Fig. 4.101 – Sumurun

Fig. 4.102 – Sumurun

Fig. 4.103 – Sumurun

Fig. 4.104 – Sumurun

Fig. 4.105 – Sumurun

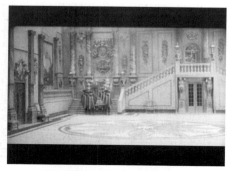

Fig. 4.106 – Madame Dubarry

Fig. 4.107 – Madame Dubarry

Fig. 4.108 -- Madame Dubarry

Fig. 4.109 – Madame Dubarry

Fig. 4.110 – Madame Dubarry

Fig. 4.111 – Madame Dubarry

Fig. 4.112 – Madame Dubarry

Fig. 4.113 – Die Flamme

Fig. 4.114 – Die Flamme

Fig. 4.115 – Die Flamme

Fig. 4.116 – Die Flamme

Fig. 4.117 – Die Flamme

Fig. 4.118 – Die Flamme

Fig. 4.119 – Die Flamme

Fig. 4.120 – Die Flamme

Fig. 4.121 – Die Flamme

Fig. 4.122 – Die Flamme

Fig. 4.123 – Die Flamme

Fig. 4.124 – Die Flamme

Fig. 4.125 – Die Flamme

Fig. 4.126 – Die Flamme

Fig. 4.127 – Die Flamme

Fig. 4.128 – Die Flamme

Fig. 4.129 – Die Flamme

Fig. 4.130 – Die Flamme

Fig. 4.131 – Die Flamme

Fig. 4.132 – Die Flamme

Fig. 4.133 – Die Flamme

Fig. 4.134 – Die Flamme

Fig. 4.135 – Die Flamme

Fig. 4.136 – Die Flamme

Fig. 4.137 – Rosita

Fig. 4.138 – Rosita

Fig. 4.139 – Forbidden Paradise

Fig. 4.140 – Forbidden Paradise

Fig. 4.141 – Forbidden Paradise

Fig. 4.142 – Forbidden Paradise

Fig. 4.143 – Forbidden Paradise

Fig. 4.144 – Forbidden Paradise

Fig. 4.145 – Forbidden Paradise

Fig. 4.146 – Forbidden Paradise

Fig. 4.147 – Forbidden Paradise

Fig. 4.148 – Forbidden Paradise

Fig. 4.149 – Forbidden Paradise

Fig. 4.150 – Forbidden Paradise

Fig. 4.151 – Forbidden Paradise

Fig. 4.152 – Forbidden Paradise

Fig. 4.153 – Forbidden Paradise

Fig. 4.154 – Forbidden Paradise

Fig. 4.155 – Forbidden Paradise

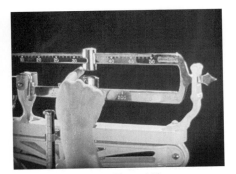

Fig. 4.156 – Three Women

Fig. 4.157 – Three Women

Fig. 4.158 – Three Women

Fig. 4.159 – Three Women

Fig. 4.160 – Three Women

Fig. 4.161 – Three Women

Fig. 4.162 – Three Women

Fig. 4.163 – Three Women

Fig. 4.164 – Three Women

Fig. 4.165 – Three Women

Fig. 4.166 – Three Women

Fig. 4.167 – Three Women

Fig. 4.168 – Three Women

Fig. 4.169 – Three Women

Fig. 4.170 – Three Women

Fig. 4.171 – Three Women

Fig. 4.172 – Three Women

Fig. 4.173 – Three Women

Fig. 4.174 – Lady Windermere's Fan

Fig. 4.175 – Lady Windermere's Fan

Fig. 4.176 – Forbidden Paradise

Fig. 4.177 – Forbidden Paradise

Fig. 4.178 – Forbidden Paradise

Fig. 4.179 – Forbidden Paradise

Fig. 4.180 – Forbidden Paradise

Fig. 4.181 – Forbidden Paradise

Fig. 4.182 – Forbidden Paradise

Fig. 4.183 – Lady Windermere's Fan

Fig. 4.184 – Lady Windermere's Fan

Fig. 4.185 – Lady Windermere's Fan

Fig. 4.186 – Lady Windermere's Fan

Fig. 4.187 – Lady Windermere's Fan

Fig. 4.188 – Lady Windermere's Fan

Fig. 4.189 – Lady Windermere's Fan

Fig. 4.190 – Lady Windermere's Fan

Fig. 4.191 – Lady Windermere's Fan

Fig. 4.192 – Lady Windermere's Fan

Fig. 4.193 – Lady Windermere's Fan

Fig. 4.194 – Lady Windermere's Fan

Fig. 4.195 – Lady Windermere's Fan

Fig. 4.196 – Lady Windermere's Fan

Fig. 4.197 – Lady Windermere's Fan

Fig. 4.198 – Lady Windermere's Fan

Fig. 4.199 – Lady Windermere's Fan

Chapter 5 Acting

Fig. 5.1 – I.N.R.I.: Die Katastrophe eines Volkes

Fig. 5.2 – I.N.R.I.: Die Katastrophe eines Volkes

Fig. 5.3 – I.N.R.I.: Die Katastrophe eines Volkes

Fig. 5.4 – I.N.R.I.: Die Katastrophe eines Volkes

Fig. 5.5 – I.N.R.I.: Die Katastrophe eines Volkes

Fig. 5.6 – I.N.R.I.: Die Katastrophe eines Volkes

Fig. 5.7 – I.N.R.I.: Die Katastrophe eines Volkes

Fig. 5.8 – I.N.R.I.: Die Katastrophe eines Volke

Fig. 5.9 – Landstrasse und Grossstadt

Fig. 5.10 – Landstrasse und Grossstadt

Fig. 5.11 – Die Ehe der Fürstin Demidoff

Fig. 5.12 – I.N.R.I.: Die Katastrophe eines Volkes

Fig. 5.13 – Landstrasse und Grossstadt

Fig. 5.14 – Meyer aus Berlin

Fig. 5.15 – Die Augen der Mumie Mâ

Fig. 5.16 – Ich möchte kein Mann sein

Fig. 5.17 – Ich möchte kein Mann sein

Fig. 5.18 – Kohlhiesels Töchter

Fig. 5.19 – Kohlhiesels Töchter

Fig. 5.20 – Sumurun

Fig. 5.21 – Die Flamme

Fig. 5.22 – Die Flamme

Fig. 5.23 – Die Flamme

Fig. 5.24 – Rosita

Fig. 5.25 – Lubitsch directing Mary Pickford and Holbrook Blinn in Rosita

Fig. 5.26 – Rosita

Fig. 5.27 – A Woman of Paris

Fig. 5.28 – The Marriage Circle

Fig. 5.29 – Lady Windermere's Fan

Fig. 5.30 – Lady Windermere's Fan

Fig. 5.31 – Lady Windermere's Fan

Fig. 5.32 – Three Women

Fig. 5.33 – Three Women

Fig. 5.34 – Three Women

Fig. 5.35 – Three Women

Fig. 5.36 – Three Women

Fig. 5.37 – Forbidden Paradise

Fig. 5.38 – Forbidden Paradise

Fig. 5.39 – So This Is Paris

Fig. 5.40 – So This Is Paris

Fig. 5.41 – So This Is Paris

Fig. 5.42 – So This Is Paris

g. 5.43 – The Student Prince in Old Heidelberg

Fig. 5.44 – The Student Prince in Old Heidelberg

ig. 5.45 – The Student Prince in Old Heidelberg

Fig. 5.46 – The Student Prince in Old Heidelberg

Fig. 5.47 – The Student Prince in Old Heidelberg

Fig. 5.48 – The Student Prince in Old Heidelberg

Chapter 6   Mutual Influences

Fig. 6.1 – Eifersucht

Fig. 6.2 – Eifersucht

Fig. 6.3 – Eifersucht

Fig. 6.4 – Eifersucht

Fig. 6.5 – Eine anständige Frau

Fig. 6.6 – Eine anständige Frau

Fig. 6.7 – Die letzte Droschke von Berlin

Fig. 6.8 – Die letzte Droschke von Berlin

Fig. 6.9 – Das Mann im Feuer

Fig. 6.10 – Das Mann im Feuer

Fig. 6.11 – Das Panzergewolbe

Fig. 6.12 – Das Panzergewolbe

Fig. 6.13 – Das Panzergewolbe

Fig. 6.14 – Daddy-Long-Legs

Fig. 6.15 – Hurrah! Ich lebe!

Fig. 6.16 – Heimkehr

Fig. 6.17 – Heimkehr

Fig. 6.18 – Heimkehr

Fig. 6.19 – Die wunderbare Lüge der Nina Petrowna

Fig. 6.20 – Die wunderbare Lüge der Nina Petrowna

Fig. 6.21 – Coeur fidèle

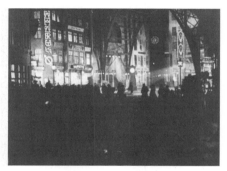

Fig. 6.22 – Sylvester

Fig. 6.23 – Sylvester

Fig. 6.24 – Der letzte Mann

Fig. 6.25 – Der letzte Mann

Fig. 6.26 – Variété

Fig. 6.27 – Hurrah! Ich Lebe!!

Fig. 6.28 – Flesh and the Devil

Fig. 6.29 – Flesh and the Devil

Fig. 6.30 – Broadway

Fig. 6.31 – Broadway

Fig. 6.32 – Wings

Fig. 6.33 – The Student Prince in Old Heidelberg

Fig. 6.34 – The Student Prince in Old Heidelberg

Fig. 6.35 – Die Strasse

Fig. 6.36 – Vom Täter fehlt jede Spur

Fig. 6.37 – Das Mann im Feuer

Fig. 6.38 – Eine anständige Frau

Fig. 6.39 – So This Is Paris

Fig. 6.40 – So This Is Paris

Fig. 6.41 – Flesh and the Devil

Fig. 6.42 – Sunrise

Fig. 6.43 – The Last Warning

Fig. 6.44 – Lonesome

Fig. 6.45 – Der letzte Mann

Fig. 6.46 – Metropolis

Epilogue   The Lubitsch Touch

Fig. E.1 – Lady Windermere's Fan

Fig. E.2 – Lady Windermere's Fan

Fig. E.3 – Lady Windermere's Fan

Fig. E.4 – Lady Windermere's Fan

in fact built inside an existing building), though the domestic settings conformed more closely to the ideals of typical Warners' sets. The dressing room of the heroine (Fig. 3.42) employs draperies to suggest a rich interior. Here a doorway, three large gathered drapes, the ubiquitous chandelier, and a few pieces of furniture combine to portray a large upper-class room. Similarly, the caddish hero's apartment where he plans to seduce the heroine's daughter is represented by a large swath of drapery and two corkscrew columns framing a dining table. The columns are flanked by a large but uninteresting tapestry that serves to set off the suggestive daybed and less conspicuous chair that define the space in the foreground (Fig. 3.43). As usual, a lamp hangs into the visible space from the unseen ceiling. Figure 3.44 shows a large nightclub set; the drapes that create a scalloped frame in the foreground and the softer, brighter background directly imitate the influential tango-bar setting from THE FOUR HORSEMEN OF THE APOCALYPSE (Fig. 3.7).

Lubitsch made another foray into the arena of historical epic when he was loaned out to Paramount in 1924 for FORBIDDEN PARADISE, his Hollywood reunion with Pola Negri. The surviving film is incomplete, but the impressively stylized set designs are readily apparent in what remains. The great designer Hans Dreier, obviously attempting to approximate contemporary German Expressionist films, created an imaginary country based on the Russia of Catherine the Great. Most of the interiors are fairly conventional sets, but for the spectacle scenes, Dreier supplied vast spaces with heavy, convoluted pillars and grotesque decorative statues (Fig. 3.45). Judging by the surviving version of the film, the result is perhaps closest to DIE BERGKATZE, but with the stylization used only sporadically.

The sets of Lubitsch's next extant Warner Bros. film, LADY WINDERMERE'S FAN are more monumental than those of his previous films at that studio. They were designed by Harold Grieve, who worked primarily as the art director for the Marshall Neilan Studios. Grieve, like Ballin and others, advocated simplicity. Shortly after completing LADY WINDERMERE in 1926, he wrote an article describing his own style and offered LADY WINDERMERE as his example: "As a rule I find that three to five pieces of furniture are sufficient for dressing a set, in which there is to be gripping dramatic action. They easily form a beautiful composition and leave plenty of space for the actors. Such a background readily recedes before the drama of the story."[22] In Figure 3.46, the area around the main door of Mrs. Erlynne's study demonstrates Grieve's approach. As with most of the rooms in this film, the walls consist of plain paneling, and the walls contain few hangings or other decorations. A small table to the right of the door, another glimpsed in the hall, and a bouquet of flowers at the lower right, fail to draw substantial attention away from Mrs. Erlynne at her desk to the left or from Lord Windermere entering. Mrs. Erlynne's hallway conveys the usual sense of a large, sparsely decorated, virtually empty space. The same is true in So This is Paris (1926), also designed by Grieve.

Grieve goes on to explain that this type of design did not aim primarily at realism, and he draws an example from The Skyrocket (1926, a Peggy Hopkins Joyce romance set in Hollywood; Grieve designed this film after Lady Windermere's Fan and before So This is Paris.) His discussion seems largely applicable to his two Lubitsch films as well:

> The day of sets for sets' sake is passed. For a successful picture, there must be co-ordination of a most intimate nature between sets and story, for the sets must help get over the feeling of the story. Mere realism or beauty alone is not sufficient. The sets must be built to harmonize with the intention of the director. They must always remain in the background, but they must fit the plot just as exactly as paper fits the wall of a room.
>
> To accomplish this end, at times it is necessary to construct an extravagant sort of set. For instance, in Skyrocket to express the type of movie dinner party which the world considers inseparable from Hollywood high society, I had to create a dining salon extreme enough to pull the spectator's eyes along the cartoonist's dotted line to the great marble pillars, the Arc de Triumphe [sic] doorways, the extravagant floral bankings, and the theatrical table appointments. An excess of vertical lines in the pillars, in the archways, in the height of the candles, all contributed to a feeling of magnificence and *je ne sais quoi* on the part of the spectator. Meanwhile, however, the huge arch at the end of the room was also designed to point with lordly gesture to Peggy Hopkins Joyce as the cynosure of my composition. But once the effect was created and the type of scene established the set had served its purpose and it immediately faded into the background for the dramatic conflict between the naive little blonde and the gentleman who was educating her.[23]

Grieve's notion of an "excess" in the vertical lines of pillars and arches seems especially appropriate to the tall rooms of Lady Windermere (Fig. 3.47). Again we see here the simplicity of the wall paneling and the use of a few pieces of furniture to dress a large set. (Do people this wealthy own no paintings?) Perhaps most remarkably, the huge doors suggest luxury while avoiding a cluttered set. Like the "tall candles" Grieve included in The Skyrocket, these doors are hardly practical; at one point Lady Windermere has to tug gracelessly to close her sitting-room door (Fig. 3.48). Placing the diminutive actor May McAvoy in such looming spaces drew at least one reviewer's attention: "Lady Windermere in more than one scene looks so small that the door knob is on a level with her head."[24] Other sets in this film demonstrate how the designs can quickly establish the upper-class milieu without drawing the eye away from the action. The ballroom set initially consists of little more than a dark, paneled wall, a few chandeliers, and two almost imperceptible pillars.

(Of course we see more of this set in later shots, including some discreet tapestries that show that the Windermeres do own some artworks.) Lord Darlington's room is similar, again with tiny lamps on tall paneled walls, peripherally placed chairs, and a chandelier.

So This is Paris takes place in a less wealthy milieu, but its characters live in scaled-down versions of the same kinds of sets. Their hallways are plain and sparsely furnished, as we see when the doctor calls on his neighbors (Fig. 3.49). The main couple's sitting room rather resembles Mrs. Erlynne's in its main elements (Fig. 3.50). Grieve's interest in tall sets resurfaces in the giant art-deco nightclub where the Artists' Ball takes place.

The Warners films demonstrate Lubitsch's successful adaptation to a new approach to set design. By the early 1920s, this approach had become recognized as the conventional way to make quality films. In 1924, the *New York Times* reviewed Lubitsch's third American film, Three Women, and described the sets in terms very similar to those we have heard from the Hollywood practitioners: "The settings of this picture, while ambitious in some scenes, are never so extravagant that they detract from the expression and actions of the players."[25] Indeed, so standardized were the designs that, as we have seen, there is a certain repetitiousness within the decors. Because the sets are so self-effacing, however, such repetitions are hardly noticeable.

The Student Prince in Old Heidelberg, Lubitsch's only silent film made at MGM, was a big-budget project. The designs for the sets in some ways exaggerated Grieve's "vertical" approach in Lady Windermere's Fan. The interiors are again tall, simple sets, but the proportions of the hero's palace are immense, and the floor is usually made more prominent by a shiny, patterned surface, as in the hero's office (Fig. 3.51). MGM was perhaps the studio most inclined to use glass shots, forced perspective, and miniatures to extend large settings, and in the beer-garden exteriors of The Student Prince, a castle on a bluff opposite the inn is created by such special effects (Fig. 3.52). In this case we are fortunate to have a fairly detailed eyewitness description of the set by a German reporter:

> I came into the Metro-Goldwyn studio on the day when the Duke of Karlsburg was supposed to die. Lubitsch was shooting the "Old Heidelberg" film, and the great backlots in Culver City looked like a part of romantic Germany. The principal residence city Karlsburg is there, charming and bourgeois and cozy; and the Heidelberg Castle, built only in the studio, in a great hangar, a Heidelberg Castle reduced by perspective, but entirely formed, with every tree leaf visible, and, behind a triple scrim of kite-mesh, looking enormously authentic and romantic.[26]

In some ways THE STUDENT PRINCE takes the elaborate settings of Lubitsch's German historical epics and tones them down; impressive as they are, they never distract from the narrative action.

Lubitsch's Work with His Hollywood Art Directors

There is, I think, one more reason Lubitsch was able to adapt so thoroughly and so successfully to filmmaking in Hollywood. He began his career by working on films intensively at all stages from planning through editing. He collaborated with the scenarist, the art director, the actors, and the cinematographer; he cut the films himself. Throughout his Hollywood career, Lubitsch participated in every stage of filmmaking to a greater extent than almost any other director. He was famous in both countries for having the film entirely visualized when filming began. In 1922, a *Photoplay* reporter observed the production of DIE FLAMME:

> Before he turns a camera upon the production, however, every detail of the story has been charted and all the research work has been completed by the art director. In col-. laboration with Lubitsch the scenarioist [sic] has turned the story into continuity. I saw the bulky script lying in state on a table some distance from the "set." Lubitsch never went near it. It was like a lovely white corpse, awaiting final disposition. Yet every detail of that scenario was being observed as scrupulously as the last wishes of the dead. Lubitsch does not improvise as many directors do. Chaplin, for instance, starts with a seed which gradually germinates. Lubitsch has written the story in carbon on his mind, every phrase is indelible.[27]

In Hollywood, directors were not usually allowed to work closely with all the major technicians at every stage of filming. Lubitsch was allowed to edit his own films only because he had such a high reputation when he arrived and continued in a position of relatively great power because of this prestige.

Yet, even Lubitsch did not have as much control under the Hollywood system as he had had in Germany. In 1929, he made this revealing comparison between art direction in Germany and in Hollywood; in Europe, he observed,

> the art-director is responsible for everything about the set; one man designs it, supervises its construction, paints it, and dresses it. Our art-directors there are a much more intimate part of the production than they are here – they are right with the picture from start to finish, even being on the set with us while we are shooting, ready to make any repairs or alterations that may be needed. Over here, there is a separate man for all of these duties – a separate mind to integrate the original design in his own way. Only once over here have I been able to have my art director work through

the picture with me as we did in Europe; that was in LADY WINDERMERE'S FAN, a picture which I think had the most perfect sets of any I have made.[28]

Arguably LADY WINDERMERE'S FAN is Lubitsch's greatest silent film, but even if one does not agree with that assessment, the sets are unquestionably among the finest from this period of his work. This description by Lubitsch of his collaborations with German and American art directors, however, suggests that he adapted to adhering to American routines (shooting without the art director present) yet continued to strive to work in the German way as much as possible. Unlike most émigré directors, he seems to have struck a happy balance between the strengths he brought with him and the rigid, though technically rich, system offered to him by Hollywood.

4 Guiding the Viewer's Attention: Editing

Lubitsch the Editor

Figure 4.1 offers a rare glimpse of Lubitsch in the editing room, working in 1922 on DIE FLAMME. This scene was obviously posed for the publicity camera, but it serves to indicate how very little equipment was involved in this stage of filmmaking. Editors in Hollywood, had by this point already rigged up small viewers by cannibalizing old cameras and projectors. The first regular sales of the Moviola editing machine began in 1924.[1] During the post-war years, however, Germans edited by eye, just as Lubitsch and his colleagues are shown doing here.

In Germany, labor was divided differently than it was in the US. In Hollywood, from the mid-1910s onward, there was a separate editor who often had assistants. The introduction of this new specialist arose largely because of the standardization of the feature film in 1915-1916. But although features became common in Germany from the early 1910s on, the role of chief editor remained with the director.[2] Assembly began with assistants cutting the camera rolls into individual shots and labeling them. After the director chose which takes to use, another assistant spliced them together into a scene. This assistant, seen in Figure 4.1 at the left, was usually female, and she was termed *die Kleberin* (literally "the gluer").

We are also fortunate to have a vivid contemporary description of Lubitsch at work in the editing room in a 1922 *Photoplay* article by an American journalist who observed part of the making of DIE FLAMME. The author has been discussing Lubitsch's great energy on the set during filming, and he goes on to discuss his behavior in the editing room:

> If Lubitsch is a fast stepper on the "set," he certainly is a shimmie dancer in the cutting room. You would imagine he was mad at the film. He tears at it until you almost think you hear him growl. Now and then he holds it up to the light and gives a blink – swish, crackle, zip – and another five hundred feet goes a-reeling. "The Flame of Love," the Negri picture he just finished, required about three days to cut and assemble. Any other director I've ever observed would take two weeks for an ordinary program feature. "The Love of Pharaoh," originally in ten or twelve reels, required less than a week.
>
> This faculty for rapid cutting must be attributed to a supernatural memory, one which carries the story so perfectly that lightning decisions are possible. Some directors spend as much time assembling a picture as upon photographing it, for it is generally conceded that this part of the production is of vital importance.[3]

I suspect that the writer is talking about European directors and their partici-
pation in the editing process.

Such absorption and skill were not just a display for a visiting fan magazine
writer. Lubitsch was clearly committed to editing his films himself, since he
continued to do so in the US. There the studio executives would have expected
Lubitsch to turn his footage over to a chief editor for this stage of filmmaking.
Indeed, even into the sound era, when the editing process became more complicated, Lubitsch edited his own films. Gottfried Reinhardt (Max's son), who
worked briefly with Lubitsch on DESIGN FOR LIVING (1933), recalled in an interview: "He really did everything himself. He even cut the film himself; he
may have been the only one who did that. I never met any director who actually went into the cutting room with scissors and cut their own films but
Lubitsch."[4] Lubitsch took his work habits with him to Hollywood, and presumably because he was so highly regarded, he was allowed to continue the
methods he had used in Germany. Consequently, the cutting patterns in both
his German and American films directly reflect his changing knowledge of the
two nations' editing norms.

By 1917, the guidelines of the classical Hollywood system for continuity editing were fully in place. In contrast, during the 1910s, Germany (and most of
Europe) had developed a rough or loose version of continuity editing. Most
European filmmakers gradually adopted cut-ins within scenes; shot/reverse
shot was not rare by 1920; and there were contiguity cuts to nearby spaces.
Apart from consistent screen direction, most of the techniques of continuity
editing were employed, but not as frequently or as smoothly as in Hollywood.

There were several aspects to the roughness of continuity practice in Germany. For one thing, German directors simply cut less often than their American peers. By 1917, Hollywood films typically began a scene with an establishing view and then quickly moved in for analytical shots to direct the
spectator's attention to the most salient narrative information from moment to
moment. Scenes in German films of the post-war era tended to stay with the
long shot until some major action or character expression motivated cutting in
– and some scenes are played without closer views. Moreover, cutting sometimes seemed more arbitrary, at least to a spectator accustomed to the continuity system. It is not always clear why some scenes move to a closer view when
they do, or why they shift back to the long shot. That is, the cutting is often not
tailored as closely to the narrative action as it is in Hollywood.

Most notably, much less attention is paid to smooth continuity at the cuts.
Matching from one shot to the next is usually more approximate than in Hollywood films - to the point where smooth matches in German films seem to occur by chance rather than by design. By the end of the 1910s, Hollywood practitioners were expected to make close matches on position and action, though

not all succeeded. But German films often contained numerous mismatches. These were not usually enough to be confusing or even necessarily noticeable - at least, presumably not to German audiences of the period (though *I* often jumped about a foot in the air at some of these cuts).

Furthermore, continuity cuts often involved considerable ellipses. A character might be seen exiting a second-floor room, and a straight cut moves to an exterior with the character already coming out the ground-floor door. There was no attempt to cover such temporal gaps by titles, cutaways, or other techniques a Hollywood film would be likely to employ. Similarly, as I probably a matter of pure chance. Shot/reverse-shot editing, cut-ins, and contiguity cuts all violated screen direction fairly frequently. In most cases this is not a problem, since we can still follow the narrative action. But occasionally, spatial relations do become baffling – especially when cuts depend on eyeline matches between two areas not seen together in an establishing shot.

Essentially, most German filmmakers seemed content to stage the action in such a way that it was visible to the spectator and to string the resulting shots together to create a reasonable sense of continuous time. Basic intelligibility was the implicit goal. In Hollywood, however, filmmakers went a step further, aiming to make spectators' comprehension of the narrative effortless by guiding their attention more precisely. Through lighting, through frequent cuts that concentrated viewer attention on small changes in the action, and especially through the principles of continuity matching, Hollywood practice aimed to make the action flow smoothly. By the early 1930s, Lubitsch would admit his own obsession with this uninterrupted flow of action.

Another sign of the differences in styles between German and Hollywood films is apparent in a new production role. In Hollywood from about 1916 on, the "script girl" was hired to sit on the set and note the positions of people and objects at the beginning and end of each take. Her purpose was to aid in the smooth flow of action at the editing stage by informing actors and director how to replicate those positions in subsequent shots. German film companies, however, did not include script girls as part of the crew. The actors, director, and cinematographer presumably kept track of such things – and they had many other things to worry about at the same time. Hence there was a lack of precisely matched shots, and this lack contributed to what I call "rough continuity."

We have seen in the two previous chapters how quickly Lubitsch assimilated Hollywood norms of lighting and set design. His adoption of continuity editing practice progressed more slowly, and we can see him gradually mastering the guidelines during the 1920s, until by LADY WINDERMERE'S FAN in 1925, he could put together an entire feature with flawless Hollywood-style editing. Clearly, his slower mastering of this particular set of stylistic techniques resulted from the fact that the editing guidelines are relatively complex, and the instantaneous changes from shot to shot cannot be studied on the screen nearly as easily as can lighting and setting.

Editing in Postwar German Films

The simplest form of analytical editing is the cut-in. It is fairly rare for a German film of this era to contain an entire scene played out without any cuts to closer views, but it did happen. In Mr. Wu (1918), for example, a scene begins with Mr. Wu entering from the rear and coming forward to join the man sitting at the left by the desk (Fig. 4.2). As the men begin to converse, there is a cut to a closer view (Fig. 4.3). The scene, however, contains no shot/reverse shots, as a Hollywood scene of this type most likely would. In the same film, a scene involving a family of four seated around a dinner table – including one with her back to the camera – is played without any change of framing (Fig. 4.4). A fairly lengthy conversation occurs, and eventually two of the characters get up and leave. The only cuts involve the insertion of intertitles, and the same framing returns after each title. Near the end of the shot, the daughter stands and moves forward to kiss her mother (Fig. 4.5). Even though this involves her moving into what I termed the dark zone in Chapter Two, there is no cut.

Most scenes, however, include cuts drawing upon several types of analytical principles. As I have suggested, violations of classical screen direction can occur in these cuts. Cut-ins tend to maintain screen direction, probably mostly because the set exists only behind the actors. The camera cannot move to the other side, since there would then be no set visible. The cameraman simply moved the camera closer to the action, generally from roughly the same vantage-point. This is evident in a particularly old-fashioned-looking scene from Die weisse Pfau. In the establishing shot (Fig. 4.6), the camera faces straight-on toward a garret set with two characters. The closer view shows them from a slightly different vantage point, to the right of the original shot, but the same curtains are visible behind them (Fig. 4.7).

Some situations, however, create the possibility of cutting in such a way as to alter screen position. In Die Ehe der Fürstin Demidoff, a typical 1910s scene staged in depth begins with a woman in the foreground left and a man entering through a door at the right rear (Fig. 4.8). His eyeline is directed left and front, toward her. In the closer view, the camera has shifted its angle so that he now looks offscreen right toward her (Fig. 4.9). In classical terms, the camera has moved across the invisible line between the two characters.

Another typical goal of Hollywood films was to match as precisely as possible the characters' positions and actions on the cut to the closer view. In practice, mismatches were not uncommon, but these were usually relatively slight and hence minimally distracting. In films employing rough continuity, the mismatches could be more flagrant. In one cut-in from ROSE BERND, there seems to have been an attempt to match the man's gesture of buttoning his coat (Figs. 4.10 and 4.11). The heroine's head, however, looks down and is in shadow in the first shot but already turned to look at the man immediately after the cut.

Lubitsch was using simple cut-ins by the time of his earliest feature films, often to emphasize facial expression or details of action. Late in ICH MÖCHTE KEIN MANN SEIN!, an establishing view of a large room (Fig. 4.12) leads to a closer view (Fig. 4.13), with the camera simply shifting straight in toward the characters, whose positions are generally matched (though the two are distinctly closer together in the medium shot). Cut-ins across the line are rare in Lubitsch's German films. One occurs in SUMURUN, where a high-angle long view of the hero and heroine in a harem (Fig. 4.14) leads to a closer view of them, not only with their screen positions switched, but also with a considerable mismatch (Fig. 4.15). The same film contains a rare double cut-in, introducing the main comic female character juggling in the harem (Figs. 4.16 to 4.18).

Contiguity cuts, showing figures moving through adjacent spaces, were more problematic for screen direction – often because they were shot outdoors without sets, and the camera could be placed on any side of the action. In Lubitsch's CARMEN, screen direction is maintained as a woman seen in one space moves rightward (Fig. 4.19) and comes into the next shot still walking rightward (Fig. 4.20). In DIE BRÜDER KARAMASSOFF, however, we see a character exiting toward the left through a doorway (Fig. 4.21), only to have him emerge into a hall in the next shot, moving rightward (Fig. 4.22). Before the transitional films of his late German period, Lubitsch was as likely as any director to construct spaces with movements that did not remain consistent at the cut. In DIE BERGKATZE, for example, the hero moves rightward as he exits the frame in one shot (Fig. 4.23), but immediately walks leftward into the nearby space (Fig. 4.24).

One of the key devices for linking spaces together from shot to shot is the eyeline of a character looking toward something offscreen. Again, whether such cuts obeyed screen direction seems to have been almost arbitrary. Some German films contained quite sophisticated uses of correct eyelines. In LANDSTRASSE UND GROSSSTADT, a famous violinist's manager wishes to seduce the musician's lover and steals up behind her in a room (Fig. 4.25). A cut-in for detail shows him kissing the back of her neck (Fig. 4.26). As the pair struggles, they move away from the camera (Fig. 4.27). A shot of a new space shows the violinist entering through a door and reacting in shock, staring off right and slightly front-presumably at the manager (Fig. 4.28). He then shifts his eyes, looking more directly off right - presumably at the wife (Fig. 4.29) - before looking right and slightly front (Fig. 4.30). We can infer from this that the manager and lover have leaped apart upon his entering, as the next shot confirms (Fig. 4.31).

Such precision, however, is rare. An otherwise fairly sophisticated series of shots from DIE WEISSE PFAU is made confusing by inconsistent eyeline direction. The heroine, a dancer, has married a rich man. As she sits at a table in a hotel cafe with her husband and friends (Fig. 4.32), she stiffens and looks off right front, wide-eyed. She has recognized her old lover, a violinist performing in the cafe. After a cut to the violinist, he stops playing and stares in shock off right. At this point in the scene, it is difficult to understand that he is supposed to be looking at the dancer (Fig. 4.33). His action is followed by a closer view of her, still looking off right front (Fig. 4.34), and another of him, as before (Fig. 4.35). By now it is clear, more from the actors' expressions than from the cutting, that they are looking at each other. A close view of the husband, who was seen sitting to the right of the dancer in the establishing shot (Fig. 4.32), shows him looking right and front (Fig. 4.36). Those who noticed him in the earlier shot will assume that he's looking at the violinist – though it would make more sense for him to look at his wife first, notice her intent gaze, and then look at her ex-lover. As the scene is presented, after looking off right (presumably at the violinist), the husband then turns his head to look at his wife, off left (Fig. 4.37). This is actually a somewhat ambitious scene for a German film of this period, trying to link three characters across a large room with eyeline matches. Failure to match the directions, however, makes us struggle to grasp where the characters are in relation to each other and at whom each is looking. It is hard to imagine an American film of this era containing a scene this confusing.

Lubitsch seems to have had some sense that maintaining screen directions in eyeline matches could be important to the understanding of a scene. The opening of DIE AUGEN DER MUMIE MÂ presents its relatively simple action through eyeline matches and a shot/reverse shot pattern. Initially we see a long shot of the hero in a desert setting, strolling down a hill and pausing to look off left front (Fig. 4.38). A long shot of a woman sitting on the edge of a well reveals what he saw. She stands up and begins to dip her jug into the water (Fig. 4.39), and a reasonably good match on this action leads to a medium-long shot. She lifts the jug to her shoulder and gazes off right front, registering alarm (Fig. 4.40). This is followed by a closer shot of the hero, staring off left front (Fig. 4.41). This leads to a medium close-up of the woman, still looking off front right, beginning to frown (Fig. 4.42). The same medium-shot framing of the poet follows as he continues to stare (Fig. 4.43). The scene returns to the long-shot view of the well as the heroine turns and moves toward the left rear, pausing to look back, then running out the left side of the frame (Fig. 4.44). The initial long-shot view of the poet returns, and he starts walking quickly toward the front left (Fig. 4.45). A cut reveals another stretch of desert. The heroine runs in from the left foreground and pauses to look back in the direction from which she had just come (Fig. 4.46). She then runs into depth and hides behind a dune. There is a return to the long-shot framing of the well, and the poet runs in from the foreground right, looks toward the left rear, where the woman had gone (Fig. 4.47), and then hurries after her. The only violation of screen direction in the scene comes when a view of a stretch of desert has the heroine running in from the foreground left when she would have to come in at the foreground right to maintain the direction of her movement from the previous time we saw her. Still, the situation is clear enough by this point that simply having her consistently moving into the depth of the shot suffices to prevent confusion.

This relatively simple example involves only two characters. Its use of eyelines and shot/reverse shot between people who are too far apart to be shown clearly in a single shot is typical of what was being used in American films beginning in the early 1910s. Lubitsch's command of eyelines was not always so clear during his German period, particularly when a group of characters was involved. A crucial scene in MADAME DUBARRY, when Louis XV first sees the heroine, Jeanne, takes place in a garden whose geography remains uncertain. Just before this moment, Jeanne has gone to Chancellor Choiseul to get her lover's debts excused. He disapproves of her and wishes to induce the King to take his own sister as his mistress, so he has ordered her out. She has left the palace and now sits disconsolately on a bench in its garden. As the crucial action begins, Louis is sitting on a similar bench among his entourage, including Choiseul's sister on his right. Louis lifts a lorgnette to his eyes and gazes off front left, as do the other men (Fig. 4.48). In the continuity system, this would establish Jeanne as offscreen left, since presumably the next shot is linked by an eyeline match rather than crosscutting: Jeanne seated on the bench (Fig. 4.49). She simply slumps despondently, apparently not seeing Louis. During this shot we will probably assume that Louis is offscreen right. That assumption would seem to be reinforced by the next shot, a closer view of Louis in which he looks again off front left – a fact that is emphasized by his odd spectacles (Fig. 4.50). Four additional tightly framed shots follow, all medium close-ups give no further information about the spatial relations: a closer shot of Jeanne sitting forlornly, another of Louis looking through his lorgnette, a shot of Choiseul's sister, looking off right at Louis in a disapproving fashion, and another shot of Louis as he lowers the lorgnette and speaks: "Such a charming encounter is a good omen for the day." After this intertitle, there is a return to the initial medium-long-shot view of the group.

Now, however, the unclear layout of the space begins to emerge. A close view of Choiseul, who had apparently been offscreen right in the general shot, shows him nodding toward the right in the course of giving an order to a servant standing at the right edge of the screen. The man exits toward the right, and Choiseul continues to look off in that direction (Fig. 4.51). The next shot presents the same framing of Jeanne's bench that we saw earlier, with the servant entering from the left to order her away (Fig. 4.52). His entrance is consistent with his rightward exit in the previous shot, but it contradicts the idea that the royal group is offscreen right from Jeanne. A re-establishing shot of the royal entourage now views the group from a different vantage-point, further leftward, with Louis looking off front right toward the bench (Fig. 4.53). The same framing of the bench now reveals it to be empty (Fig. 4.54). This scene is far more elaborate than the opening of DIE AUGEN, yet we have only slightly more trouble following the action despite the contradiction in eyeline matching. Given that the import ban was still in force, Lubitsch may have had access to some continuity-style films that were not circulated in theaters, or he may simply have become more ambitious in his editing as he gained greater experience.

Shot/reverse shot is a specific type of eyeline usage, usually involving characters framed in separate shots and facing each other. German films of this period did make use of shot/reverse shot, though in most cases far less frequently than their Hollywood counterparts would. In DIE BRÜDER KARAMASSOFF, a conversation scene follows the classical pattern of establishing shot (Fig. 4.55), cut-in to one character looking off (Fig. 4.56), and following shot of another character looking in the opposite direction (Fig. 4.57). Some directors were capable of using even more sophisticated shot/reverse shots than what we just saw in LANDSTRASSE UND GROSSSTADT. In DIE LIEBSCHAFTEN DES HEKTOR DALMORE, a duel scene uses a variety of framings, all obeying screen direction and conveying the situation quite clearly. A long shot establishes two men initially at some distance from each other and facing away from each other (Fig. 4.58). A closer shot shows one of the men from behind (Fig. 4.59). Although the camera is quite close to the 180-degree line, he faces slightly right. He turns to fire, his glance shifting toward the left foreground, where his opponent would be (Fig. 4.60). A cut reveals the hero, also seen initially from the rear (Fig. 4.61). He spins and faces off right, raising his arm (Fig. 4.62). An impressive shot past the hero's right shoulder still places him toward the left of the composition and facing right into depth, while the other man is visible to the right of the frame (Fig. 4.63); thus the cuts maintain the men's screen position in relation to each other. After a straight cut-in, the opponent fires, still facing left foreground (Fig. 4.64). In reverse shot, the hero reacts to being hit (Fig. 4.65), and a return to the previous framing leads to the opponent's reaction (Fig. 4.66).

Lubitsch made little or no attempt to observe screen direction when creating shot/reverse-shot series. Eyelines that violate screen direction are common throughout his German period. They occur in his simple rustic comedies, such as in a meeting between the hero and heroine in ROMEO UND JULIA IM SCHNEE (Figs. 4.67 and 4.68), but they crop up in his most expensive epics as well, such as in this conversation scene from ANNA BOLEYN (Figs. 4.69 and 4.70). The same film contains scenes in perfect continuity style and others executed in a confusing way. SUMURUN, for example, contains a shot/reverse-shot conversation between the heroine (looking to the right front) and another woman of the harem (looking to the left front). The segment begins with medium-long views of them both (Figs. 4.71 and 4.72), then moves in for medium close-ups partway through the scene (Figs. 4.73 and 4.74). This variety of distances within a conversation scene was quite unusual for the period. Yet elsewhere, a conversation between the head eunuch and a merchant in shot/reverse shot shows the eunuch looking off left front (Fig. 4.75) and the merchant looking directly off left (Fig. 4.76). The spatial confusion is clarified somewhat when the merchant actually moves out frame left and enters the next shot of the head eunuch moving rightward (Fig. 4.77), creating a cut between contiguous spaces that crosses the axis of action.

On the whole, Lubitsch was clearly more ambitious than most German directors in his creation of complicated scenes through editing. These might contain clumsy or ambiguous cuts, but they demonstrate the technical savvy that would soon allow Lubitsch to adopt Hollywood techniques remarkably quick.

The impressive scene in CARMEN where the heroine first sees the toreador Escamillo demonstrates this combination of ambitious and awkward editing, as if Lubitsch were pushing the conventions of the rough continuity of the day. It was typical in the European cinema of this period to stage action in depth, usually without a great deal of cutting. Here Lubitsch tries to combine depth staging with a striking, if odd, set of cut-ins and proto-shot/reverse shots.

In a medium-long shot that serves to establish the space of an outdoor café, Carmen sits at a table in the right foreground with her current lover, a soldier who is a minor character in the plot. As Escamillo moves past their table, he and Carmen exchange glances (Fig. 4.78). In close-up, she looks him up and down appraisingly (Fig. 4.79). A tight reverse shot shows him ogling her in turn (Fig. 4.80). After a second close-up of her, the scene returns to the original establishing view (Fig. 4.81). Here Carmen turns to her oblivious lover while Escamillo walks into the depth of the shot, turning to look back at her; he sits at another table. Despite the importance of this moment, Lubitsch stages the action confusingly, with a wooden pillar in the middle-ground preventing our seeing his action of sitting down. A cut-in introduces a third framing of Carmen, in medium shot, as she turns around to look at Escamillo (Fig. 4.82). Despite maintaining a considerable degree of depth, this shot does not include the space where the toreador is sitting. Carmen faces left rear, setting up a shot/reverse-shot situation. Another medium shot of Escamillo follows, as he lifts his glass to Carmen (Fig. 4.83). He looks slightly off left front, so the eyelines are mismatched by the standards of a continuity-style shot/reverse shot. Still, Lubitsch has balanced the two shots by making both of them medium views – the most common option in a shot/reverse-shot series. In the next shot of Carmen, she turns front with a fascinated expression (Fig. 4.84). A cut returns us to the establishing view, and Carmen gets up and walks into the depth of the shot, following Escamillo's earlier trajectory (Fig. 4.85). Finally, a cut-in shows the toreador's table in medium-long shot as Carmen starts to walk past it while staring at him (Fig. 4.86). Lubitsch has set up a second deep-space composition behind the initial one, as Carmen stops to wait in a hallway at the rear and Escamillo rises to follow her (Fig. 4.87). Despite the one clumsy bit of staging and the lack of adherence to the 180-degree rule, editing breaks this scene down quite precisely into a set of shots, each one contributing a distinct action to the story. This presentation of narrative information through a series of precise, relatively short shots would remain one aspect of Lubitsch's silent-film style, and exposure to Hollywood films would allow him to refine it considerably.

A shorter, less complex – but more skillfully executed – scene breakdown occurs in DIE PUPPE. The doll-maker is chasing his young apprentice, who flees to the kitchen and solicits the protection of the doll-maker's wife, then climbs out the window and threatens to jump. After the apprentice wrecks the kitchen, he exits, moving leftward, leaving the wife to help take a pot off the doll-maker's head (Fig. 4.88). A cut to the window has the apprentice enter, still moving leftward (Fig. 4.89). He climbs out and by the shot's end, he is clinging to the frame and looking back at the others, off right (Fig. 4.90). A dialogue intertitle follows: "I can't bear the disgrace; I'll jump out the window and kill myself." A reverse shot shows the wife, looking off left toward him, reacting in horror (Fig. 4.91). Lubitsch cuts back and forth between these two framings, prolonging the suspense: there is a second shot of him, a second shot of her, and finally a third shot of him. Abruptly the comic pay-off comes as Lubitsch cuts outside and shows the apprentice sliding down from the window to the ground, only inches below (Fig. 4.92).

One final example, from SUMURUN should demonstrate Lubitsch's growing skill at using eyelines and at breaking a scene down by allotting one shot per significant action. It also shows his lack of awareness of the 180-degree rule in a particularly dramatic way. A hunchback clown who heads a traveling troupe of street performers has just given the troupe's beautiful, fickle dancer a cheap bracelet. She reacts by becoming far friendlier toward him, until a handsome young merchant arrives with clothes purchased for her by the Sheik's son – at which point she turns away and ignores the hunchback. The action begins in an establishing shot as the merchant arrives and begins to show the delighted dancer some clothes while the hunchback assumes a worried expression (Fig. 4.93). During this action, Lubitsch balances the hunchback's unhappiness with the attraction the dancer feels toward the merchant, and he weaves these two lines together with close views and glances that make the emotions of all three perfectly clear. From the establishing view, Lubitsch cuts to a medium close-up of the hunchback watching the others. The closer framing emphasizes his unhappiness, which will be the main focus of this short segment (Fig. 4.94). He is staring off left toward the dancer, and an eyeline match leads to a close shot of her hand dropping the cheap bracelet (Fig. 4.95). Another quick shot shows it landing on the ground (Fig. 4.96), and the scene then returns to the Hunchback's growing despair (Fig. 4.97); his gaze shifts downward. A second close shot of the bracelet on the ground follows, and a hand reaches in from off left to pick it up (Fig. 4.98).

The sleeve might identify the hand as being that of the hunchback, but by the logic of screen direction, he should reach in from the right, since he has been established as being on the dancer's right. In the shot of the hunchback looking down, he does not move as if to pick up the bracelet, so there is no match on gesture that could cue us that the hand is his. Here is a case where screen direction is not neutral; the action is slightly confusing as a result of the violation, given that Lubitsch has chosen to string so many tight views together after the establishing shot. The next shot shifts the action briefly to the dancer, seen in medium close-up looking expectantly up and off left at the merchant (Fig. 4.99). In the reverse shot of him, however, his eyeline makes it clear that he is looking over her head at the hunchback and noticing the clown's pathetic gesture and reaction (Fig. 4.100). His eyeline matches at the cut with a new, slightly more distant framing of the hunchback, sadly holding up the discarded present (Fig. 4.101). A cut returns to the same view of the merchant, whose face saddens (Fig. 4.102); his hopeless love for Sumurun, a concubine of the Sheik, presumably makes him sensitive to another thwarted suitor's feelings. Lubitsch milks the moment's pathos by cutting again to the hunchback (Fig. 4.103) before showing the dancer again, apparently wondering why the merchant is paying so little attention to her (Fig. 4.104). The scene returns to the establishing view, and the hunchback rises and goes into the tent (Fig. 4.105). By 1919, Lubitsch was letting editing and especially eyeline matches convey much more of the narrative information, minimizing the necessity for pantomimic acting. This subtle use of eyelines in SUMURUN suggests how he accomplished this change. Indeed, this film evidences a leap forward in Lubitsch's mastery of editing.

Editing – especially continuity-style editing – is often considered the main indicator of stylistic progress within the silent period, but as I have argued elsewhere, staging within a single take developed in a highly sophisticated way in some European films of the 1910s.[5] Before moving on to Lubitsch's transitional films of 1921-22, it is worth looking at a masterful scene in MADAME DUBARRY that exemplifies Lubitsch's skill at staging and using eyelines within a long take. The action of the scene occurs after the death of Louis XV, as Choiseul, his minister, supervises soldiers carrying his coffin across a large hall. A horizontally masked establishing shot shows the procession slowly coming down the steps (Fig. 4.106). In a closer framing, the soldiers set the coffin down as Jeanne rushes in, weeping, and throws herself against it (Fig. 4.107). Choiseul, who has always strongly resented Jeanne's influence over the king, indignantly sends her away, and she exits to the left foreground (Fig. 4.108). Choiseul stands for a moment looking sternly after her (Fig. 4.109), then turns and orders the bearers to lift the coffin up again (Fig. 4.110). He stands respectfully as they move out foreground right (Fig. 4.111; note the "dark zone" through which they pass as they approach the camera). After they have all exited, however, Choiseul turns again, and the shot ends with him staring after Jeanne (Fig. 4.112). The fact that he is watching Jeanne rather than the departing coffin suggests that his hatred of her is greater than his love for his king – and indeed, he finally gives a triumphant little laugh and walks away toward the left rear as the lengthy shot ends. Here Lubitsch has masterfully conveyed the scene's actions without editing or intertitles. It is hard to imagine a Hollywood film of the 1910s handling an action like this without cutting, but Lubitsch gains the advantage of using Choiseul's glances at offscreen spaces to comment on his character.

Such extended takes are rare, however, and Lubitsch's future lay with continuity editing. His transitional films, DAS WEIB DES PHARAO and DIE FLAMME, make it clear that he consciously practiced this new approach. It is worth examining one entire scene from DIE FLAMME; no other scene in Lubitsch's surviving German work so clearly exemplifies his leap into Hollywood-style filmmaking. Note also how Lubitsch employs back-lighting throughout this scene, picking the characters out against the dark, inconspicuous setting.

Yvette, a woman with a shady reputation, has married a naïve young composer, André. His musician friend Raoul, a lecherous hypocrite, comes to visit Yvette to try to break up the marriage so that Yvette can become his mistress. Raoul is unaware that she has placed André behind some curtains to eavesdrop on their conversation. The establishing medium-long shot places her on the right and Raoul on the left, but the dark curtains behind where André is hiding are visible in the arch at the rear (Fig. 4.113). Raoul offers Yvette a letter from André's mother enclosing a check to pay her off if she leaves the young man. A cut-in shows her in medium shot holding the check and looking off left at Raoul – a direction consistent with their spatial relations in the previous shot (Fig. 4.114). In reverse medium shot, he looks confidently and expectantly off right at her (Fig. 4.115). The previous framing is repeated as she tears it up (Fig. 4.116). A cutaway to André peeking through the curtains ensures that we know he has witnessed her action (Fig. 4.117). Another medium shot shows Yvette offering the pieces of the check to Raoul (Fig. 4.118). Lubitsch now moves to a closer framing of Raoul as he looks menacingly off at Yvette (Fig. 4.119). The same medium-shot framing of her follows, as she speaks defiantly to him (Fig. 4.120). A still closer, nearly frontal shot of Raoul shows his eyes shifting away from her toward the left (Figs. 4.121 and 4.122). A dialogue title renders his line: "I am speaking here entirely on his behalf." In another medium shot, Yvette speaks tauntingly to him (Fig. 4.123), followed by her dialogue title: "Really only on his behalf?" Again in close-up, Raoul's eyes shift quickly back toward her (Figs. 4.124 and 4.125), thinking that she has realized his real motive for visiting her. Another shot of her mocking face follows (Fig. 4.126), and then one of him glancing down and away (Fig. 4.127) and immediately back toward her. Finally Lubitsch provides a closer view of her face to balance the one of Raoul (Fig. 4.128). The reverse shot of Raoul shows him beginning to get excited as he concludes that she is flirting with him (Fig. 4.129). After another close view of her grinning face (Fig. 4.130), a cut returns us to Raoul as Yvette moves into the frame from the right, leaning slightly against him as he becomes more excited (Fig. 4.131).

Following this long stretch of close framings, the scene then moves to a general view including the curtains, though the camera is slightly closer than in the opening shot (Fig. 4.132). He embraces her, and she speaks, with the following dialogue title: "You selfless friend!" The title leads directly to a closer view of the curtained screen as André angrily tosses it aside (Fig. 4.133). A completely new framing shows Yvette standing straight as Raoul turns and cowers; note how a small portion of the toppled screen intrudes into the frame at the far left, further helping to orient the viewer (Fig. 4.134). Then André appears in medium close-up (Fig. 4.135), staring angrily off right front at Raoul, shown in another medium close-up framing (Fig. 4.136).

One could easily imagine this scene in an American film of the same period. Each distinct facial expression and glance that conveys even a small amount of story detail receives a separate shot, and the resulting progression of framing guides the spectator to notice them effortlessly. At the point where the dramatic tension escalates and Yvette defies Raoul by tearing up the check,

Lubitsch moves to tighter shots of each character to create dramatic emphasis. By only about a year and a half after Hollywood films returned to German screens, Lubitsch had already absorbed the continuity approach to editing.[6]

Lubitsch's Hollywood Films

By the time Lubitsch started working in Hollywood, his films probably contained no more continuity errors than did those of American-trained directors – and probably fewer than many. In ROSITA, Lubitsch twice cuts across the line during shot/reverse-shot passages, including this exchange with both the king and Rosita looking off right front (Figs. 4.137 and 4.138).

Rather than examining Lubitsch's use of continuity principles in numerous brief scenes from his American films, it seems more useful to examine a few relatively extended passages that demonstrate his mastery of such principles and his development of a distinctive approach. I shall focus primarily on the less accessible titles, FORBIDDEN PARADISE and THREE WOMEN, before concluding with a scene from LADY WINDERMERE'S FAN, the film where Lubitsch attains utter mastery of continuity editing.

FORBIDDEN PARADISE offers a simple example of Lubitsch's sophistication. One scene that involves a number of characters initially arranged in depth on either side of a doorway contrasts interestingly with the CARMEN cafe scene (Figs. 4.78 to 4.87). Earlier Lubitsch had had a bit of trouble achieving shot/reverse shot in a deep set, but in FORBIDDEN PARADISE, he is cutting more freely around the action by creating correct, easily comprehensible eyelines. In this scene, Alexei, a young officer, has overheard some men plotting a rebellion against the Czarina, and he rushes to the palace to warn her. There he meets his fiancée, who is a lady-in-waiting. Menjou plays the prime minister, who has called in soldiers to arrest the hero. In this scene, the Czarina opens her door to find the hero and the soldiers outside.

The scene begins simply with an establishing shot placing Alexei just outside the doorway to the right, with the Czarina inside to his left (Fig. 4.139). A cut-in maintains their relative screen positions and captures her startled reaction at finding him there (Fig. 4.140). A cut to Alexei's fiancée follows. She has been established as being in the outer room, and her shocked stare provides an eyeline match with the previous shot (Fig. 4.141). In typical correct continuity fashion, this cutaway covers a move into a new space where relative spatial positions can be shifted. In the new shot, we are inside the room, with the Czarina now on the right and Alexei still in the doorway on the left; almost immediately the two soldiers appear and seize him (Fig. 4.142). A dialogue title follows: "Your Majesty! Your life and throne are at stake! Mutiny——" In medium close-up, the Czarina stares leftward at him (Fig. 4.143), then glances angrily off right (Fig. 4.144). We see a reverse medium close-up of the Chancellor, looking leftward at her and then exiting the frame, also leftward (Fig. 4.145). A medium-long shot of the Czarina follows, with the Chancellor entering immediately from the right – thus confirming all the spatial relations implied by the eyelines so far (Fig. 4.146). Another dialogue title conveys his speech: "Your majesty, please do not lose your charming smile. This gentleman is a little confused ..." In medium close-up, Alexei looks right front toward them, appearing to be upset enough to make the Chancellor's claim plausible (Fig. 4.147); the soldiers' hands are still visible on his shoulders. He speaks earnestly. Cut to a medium close-up of the Czarina, looking doubtfully between the Chancellor, off right (Fig. 4.148) and Alexei, off left (Fig. 4.149). Yet another medium close-up shows the Chancellor looking off left and making a winking signal to the soldiers (Fig. 4.150). These men become more visible again in a medium shot of Alexei staring at the Czarina and struggling as they try to drag him away (Fig. 4.151). In reverse medium close-up she imperiously says "Stop!" (Fig. 4.152; the word is quite intelligible from her lip movements, despite the lack of an intertitle). A return to Alexei and the soldiers visible in this framing show them snapping to attention (as the second soldier, who has been largely visible as a hand on Alexei's right shoulder, snaps to attention, his hand disappears from view; see Fig. 4.153). In the same two-shot framing of the Czarina and Chancellor seen earlier, she gestures for Alexei to enter (Fig. 4.154). This little segment culminates with a long shot of the door from inside as Alexei enters the Czarina's room and she slams the door shut in the soldiers' faces (Fig. 4.155). Thus Lubitsch has dealt with a situation staged in depth, using a string of correctly handled eyelines; he has covered a cut across the 180-degree line with a cutaway; and he has neatly book-ended his scene with long shots of Alexei seen from either side of the same doorway.

Lubitsch's skill at telling a story visually is perhaps most famously displayed in the opening of THE MARRIAGE CIRCLE, where Professor Stock's glances compare his own nearly empty dresser drawer with his wife's full one. This and other details establish the shaky state of the couple's marriage without resorting to intertitles. A briefer but equally effective scene opens his next film, THREE WOMEN. The surviving print of THREE WOMEN has no introductory intertitle. It is doubtful that the original film began so abruptly, since other Lubitsch films have opening intertitles. Nevertheless, the sequence's action is so clearly laid out in a short series of shots that it could certainly do without one; if there was an opening title, it may have been a generalization rather than a lead-in to the specific scene.

A close-up of the balance of some scales against a black background shows a woman's hands adjusting the weights slowly upward, as if she does not believe what they reveal (Fig. 4.156). A cut back to a medium shot reveals Mabel, one of the three women of the title, standing on the scales and looking down in disappointment (Fig. 4.157). Hands reach in from offscreen to drape a robe over her shoulders (Fig. 4.158). A cut moves us to a new space, a long shot of a large room, expensively decorated. Mabel walks into it from the foreground left (moving in silhouette through a deliberately created "dark zone" into the brightly lit room; see Fig. 4.159). She sits at a dressing table at the right rear, and a maid enters from off left, wheeling a table with a meal laid out on it (Fig. 4.160). A cut-in moves us close enough to see a lavish breakfast, and Mabel gestures for the maid to take it away (Fig. 4.161). As the maid begins to depart, however, Mabel calls her back and reaches for something on the table; a close shot then reveals her picking up a slice of grapefruit (Fig. 4.162). In medium shot, she takes a tiny bite, winces at its sourness (Fig. 4.163) and then takes another nibble. Thus a desire to stave off the effects of aging is set up as a major trait for this central character.

The best-known example of Lubitsch's virtuoso ability to unite a dispersed group of people through a series of eyeline matches appears in the racetrack scene in LADY WINDERMERE'S FAN. Various individuals and groups are surveying the infamous Mrs. Erlynne through their binoculars, all with different motives and reactions.[7] We can, however, see Lubitsch exploring this same territory – with distinctly less sophistication – in the second sequence from THREE WOMEN, a large charity ball. After a short series of distant views establishes the overall space and shows crowds of revelers, Lubitsch concentrates on a major character, the caddish spendthrift Lamont. In medium shot, a cigarette girl and a female partygoer stare in fascination off right, followed by a dialogue title, "That is Mr. Lamont!", and a return to the two-shot (Fig. 4.164). An eyeline match to Lamont follows; he is initially looking off left front, as if in shot/reverse shot with the two women (Fig. 4.165). He then glances off right front (Fig. 4.166). This leads to a medium-long shot of three other women, also talking, smiling, and staring off right front (Fig. 4.167). There is no shot of Lamont at this point, but rather a cut to a medium shot of two different women, also looking just off right front and smiling (Fig. 4.168). By this point in the scene it is clear enough that all these women are looking at Lamont, but whether he sees any of them remains ambiguous. I suspect that the ambiguity concerning Lamont's glances in this scene has not been deliberately created by Lubitsch, since the main effect is simply confusion concerning what he sees.

This ambiguity carries into the next shot of Lamont, looking off right front (Fig. 4.169) as at the end of the previous shot of him. He shifts his gaze just slightly more directly off right (Fig. 4.170). It is not clear whether he is looking at the space shown in the next shot, where a group of men – not looking at Lamont – are seen in medium-long shot (Fig. 4.171). A brief series of shots then shows two actions: the men discuss Lamont's debts, and Lamont casually tosses money about as he buys large numbers of corsages from a group of women. As Lamont looks off left front, his smile fades (Fig. 4.172), and a reverse shot shows his main creditor watching his profligacy with annoyance (Fig. 4.173).

This last pair of shots finally makes it clear that Lamont had not previously been looking off at these men (Fig. 4.170), since they were offscreen left at that point. Presumably he had not been looking at any of the women either. Instead, as in the LADY WINDERMERE racetrack scene, one person is observed by many without his returning their gazes. But by LADY WINDERMERE, Lubitsch has learned how better to indicate directions of gazes, and the binocular masks cue us very clearly that Mrs. Erlynne is not looking at any of those ogling or gossiping about her (as in Figs. 4.174 and 4.175).

Lubitsch developed a variant of analytical editing which, though not unique to his films, was used more systematically there than in other filmmakers' work. We might describe this as a triangular space: an area defined by shifting eyelines and character movement, with the camera remaining within a roughly triangular area for all its positions, facing outward in various directions to capture the ongoing action. I shall look at a simple example from FORBIDDEN PARADISE, followed by a more extended and complex scene in LADY WINDERMERE.

Late in FORBIDDEN PARADISE, after the rebellion against the Czarina has been foiled, she has Alexei (who has become her lover) arrested. This segment begins with the Czarina pressing a button on her desk, looking front and just barely to the right of the camera (Fig. 4.176). The reverse medium-long shot shows the door, with two officers entering and looking diagonally off left at her (Fig. 4.177). In a brief medium close-up, the Czarina now looks almost directly front at the off-screen Alexei (Fig. 4.178) before shifting her glance back to the right and the soldiers (Fig. 4.179) and speaking. A title follows: "Catch him!" (probably something more like "Seize him!" in the original). The next shot returns to the same framing of her, still looking right (Fig. 4.180) before again glancing front at Alexei (Fig. 4.181). Finally we see Alexei, facing frontally into the camera in a medium-long shot from her point of view; the two officers enter from the left to arrest him (Fig. 4.182). Despite the simplicity of this arrangement, Lubitsch has carefully placed the camera directly on the line between the Czarina and Alexei for their shot/reverse shots, intensifying their to-camera glances. He films the soldiers in Figure 4.182 from within the triangle, making them less important to the action and concentrating the spectator's attention on the interplay between the lovers.

This scene involves three points occupied by characters, but in LADY WINDERMERE, Lubitsch has mastered this combination of staging and editing to create a more complex, shifting triangular space with only two characters. He permits glances and movements between doors and pieces of furniture to convey the nuances of the developing action. Lord Windermere has come to call on Mrs. Erlynne, and he learns that she is his wife's disgraced mother. This is the first time we have seen her sitting room, which is revealed gradually in the course of the action rather than in a single distant establishing view.

The establishing shot that does begin the scene shows only a portion of the room. Mrs. Erlynne sits in the right middle ground at a desk, worrying about large unpaid bills. In the same shot, the maid announces and then admits Windermere through the large centered door at the rear (Fig. 4.183). The maid exits and closes the door as Mrs. Erlynne rises and moves right and rearward to greet her guest (Fig. 4.184). A cut-in maintains their respective positions as she continues her rightward movement (Fig. 4.185), introduces herself, and gestures politely off right front (Fig. 4.186). An eyeline match shows a small sofa by a window (Fig. 4.187). A return to a slightly closer framing of the two shows him refusing her invitation to sit. He pulls a letter out of his pocket, and she nods to acknowledge that she wrote it. A dialogue title interrupts the shot as he asks, "Who are you – and what does this letter mean?" In the same two-shot framing, he continues to question her, then glances off left (Fig. 4.188). A point-of-view shot shows a magazine photograph of Lady Windermere, which we had seen Mrs. Erlynne place there before he came in (Fig. 4.189). Again in medium shot, he questions her further, and she replies: "I am the mother of your wife."

A return to the same medium framing shows Windermere reacting with surprise, then glancing around the room, first toward the main door (Fig. 4.190) and then off right front (Fig. 4.191). A cut reveals another door across the room, with the right edge of the window seen in Figure 4.187 visible at the left edge of the frame, suggesting that the sofa is just offscreen in that direction. Windermere immediately enters from off left front (Fig. 4.192) and moves to look outside the door and close it, turning back to face Mrs. Erlynne, off left front (Fig. 4.193). In reverse medium close-up, she responds with an amused look, facing right front (Fig. 4.194). In a closer framing than before, he says (with no intertitle but quite clearly from the actor's lip movements) "I don't believe it."

At this point the pivot shots of the last part of the triangular space occurs, as she moves back to her desk (Figs. 4.195 and 4.196), walking right to left in both. She looks off left at him as she speaks: "I knew you would doubt me – here are the proofs of my identity." A medium reverse shot of him reveals him now looking off right front, with his eyeline completing the triangle that began with her sitting at the desk (Fig. 4.197). A return to a slightly more distant view of the desk shows him moving in from the left (Fig. 4.198) and sitting down to look at the documents as Mrs. Erlynne moves to the left (Fig. 4.199). Thus the trajectory of Windermere's bafflement, surprise, worry, doubt, and resignation is played out in a deceptively simple fashion.

By this point, it seems safe to say that Lubitsch had nothing more to learn from Hollywood, but Hollywood could still learn from a filmmaker who had arrived less than three years earlier. In the *Moving Picture World*'s review of THREE WOMEN, the writer commented on "the delightful touches of comedy, the power to register his points by short and constantly changing scenes [i.e., shots] and shots [framings?] focused on exceedingly limited areas [i.e., of the sets], all the while preserving excellent continuity."[8] Reviews of the time seldom mentioned editing in any director's films, so there seems little doubt that Lubitsch's virtuoso employment of continuity impressed some knowledgeable viewers. As with lighting and setting, he was more introspective about his editing techniques than most of his American counterparts. Perhaps he, as an editor, was unusually aware of what sort of footage he, as a director, had to provide in order to have shots cut together smoothly. Perhaps his thorough knowledge of the technical aspects of filmmaking allowed him to appreciate the specific editing techniques in the work of other filmmakers whom he admired.

In 1932, Lubitsch published an essay on directing films. He has been describing how important it is to plan every detail in a film in advance, especially because the shots are photographed out of continuity order:

> How vital it is, then, for every scene, every action, to be detailed down to the very last raising of an eyelid. If I were to go into the studio with only a hazy idea of how I was going to treat the subject, muddle and chaos would result. At least it would in my case, although different people have different ways of working ...
>
> A film should appear, when it is completed, to have been "shot" from beginning to end in one complete piece. That, as you will understand, can seldom be achieved in fact; but careful preparation can give the impression of a complete whole.[9]

We have already seen how Lubitsch did indeed prepare every detail and arrive at the set with a complete conception of the film in his mind. Such thoroughness, combined with a phenomenal memory, meant that the footage he sent to the editing room could easily be cut together to give the impression of action flowing smoothly from beginning to end.

5 Peeking at the Players: Acting

The Survival of Pantomimic Acting in Post-War German Cinema

Film historians commonly distinguish between pantomimic acting, which relies on the stance and movements of the body as a whole, from facially oriented acting, which is generally associated with closer framings. The facial style developed in tandem with the formulation of the continuity editing system. The basic assumption of that system is that a scene should be broken up into an establishing shot and a series of closer shots which guide the attention of the spectator effortlessly to the most salient portions of the space. To preserve clarity, the shots should be joined with matched action and screen direction.

In *The Classical Hollywood Cinema,* I have described how pantomimic acting dominated early filmmaking internationally and how Hollywood began its transition to the facial style during the period 1911-1913. At the time, the approach was explicitly referred to as "the American style."[1] Acting with the body never disappeared, of course. Actors learned to adjust the broadness of their gestures depending on whether they were framed in long shot or close-up. Slapstick comedy continued to depend more on pantomimic acting than most other genres did.

Most European national cinemas did not adopt this American system of staging and editing scenes until the 1920s. During the early 1910s, the best European directors became adept at staging intricate series of actions in different planes within a relatively deep setting.[2] The best known exemplar of this style as it was used in Germany is Franz Hofer, whose main work appeared in the years just before Lubitsch began working exclusively in features.[3]

Thus pantomimic acting continued to hold sway over most European film industries. Actors also tended to display exaggerated facial expressions, so as to be visible in medium-long or long-shot framings. Such acting was developed along different lines in Italy, Russia, and Sweden, where it became an important element in their rapidly developing national styles during the early to mid-1910s.

Why did a comparable development toward a distinctive national style not take place in Germany? Perhaps the high demand for new directors attracted recruits from the theatre, many of whom stuck with pantomimic acting. Most actors also came from the theatre and continued to divide their time between the two arts. Their presence may have fostered an old-fashioned acting style, especially when compared with the most vibrant national cinemas of the war period. Even experienced film actors were used to performing to a distant camera, and continued to use the same style even after the framing became closer.

A clear example of old-fashioned "diva" acting, with all its information pantomimed by the actors in a single lengthy shot with a distant framing, occurs in I.N.R.I.: DIE KATASTROPHE EINES VOLKES (1920). In a scene staged in an upper-class setting, a successful actress rejects her ex-lover's request to resume their affair. As the shot begins, they stand close together, and he leans toward her and holds her hand; she leans away from him (Fig. 5.1). As he takes a step back, she withdraws her hand, and he immediately grabs her wrist (Fig. 5.2). She then thrusts his hand away and makes a gesture of rejection; he stands leaning slightly toward her, holding his hat; his legs are apart, as if he might either leave or move toward her to renew his pleas (Fig. 5.3). Slowly he moves his feet together, standing more upright (Fig. 5.4). After pausing uncertainly, he walks out right (Fig. 5.5). As he departs she lowers her head, and once he has exited, she puts her right arm up to her head (Fig. 5.6), turns, lowers her arm, walks to the window, and pulls the curtain aside (Fig. 5.7). Only then does a cut-in provide a close-up as she lowers the curtain and looks at the camera with a sad, weary expression (Fig. 5.8).

The long shot in Figures 5.1 through 5.7 recalls the virtuoso passages of acting typical of Italian diva films from the mid-1910s, and comparable Russian melodramas from the same era, where slow pacing and psychologically intense performances were the fashion.[4] Similar effects could be accomplished in closer framings. In Figures 5.9 and 5.10, from LANDSTRASSE UND GROSSSTADT, Conrad Veidt demonstrates his patented suffering expression, aided by two of the most flexible eyebrows ever to grace the screen. By the late 1910s, however, the dwindling Italian film industry and the Soviet Revolution had curtailed these trends, and passages of acting by means of a slow series of poses and gestures looked decidedly old-fashioned. This acting style contributed to the reputation of German post-war silent films' as slow-paced.

Looks into the lens like the one in Figure 5.8 above are fairly common in all genres of German film during this era, while in Hollywood they had been largely banished except in comedies. A similar moment occurs in another drama, DIE EHE DER FÜRSTIN DEMIDOFF (1921), along with a display of broad facial acting. Early in the film, the wealthy and elderly Demidoff arranges with an impoverished noblewoman to wed her pretty young daughter; after a shot/reverse-shot exchange across a table, a medium close-up shows Demidoff glancing sideways at the camera as if to acknowledge his sly villainy (Fig. 5.11). In general, German cinema tended to use exaggerated gestures and facial expressions for some years after they had been toned down in Hollywood.

In I.N.R.I.: Die Katastrophe eines Volkes, two men expressing emotion look more like they are wrestling (Fig. 5.12). Fritz Kortner, one of the great actors of the Expressionist stage, competes with Veidt in chewing the scenery in Landstrasse und Grossstadt (Fig. 5.13). It is possible that performances like these were simply more to German tastes, although more moderate styles of acting quickly emerged in the wake of American influence in the 1920s.

Lubitsch's German Features

Lubitsch had been trained within the German theatre tradition, and indeed he continued to work on the stage at night until late 1918.[5] Moreover, he had emphasized slapstick comedy for much of his career, as his last film portrayals of the popular comic character Meyer amply demonstrate (Fig. 5.14). He continued to direct comedies until 1921, though these were hardly romantic comedies in the Hollywood sense. All of his comedies included romances, but they were broad and farcical in style, from the Ossi Oswalda vehicles to the two Bavarian Shakespeare travesties of 1920 to Die Bergkatze. Jan-Christopher Horak has suggested how Lubitsch modified his approach to acting in these comedies:

> By using actors whose comic personae were well established on the screen, Lubitsch's characters remain thoroughly human in their madness. Both Oswalda and [Harry] Liedtke, as well as [Victor] Janson play characters which they had developed in countless other films. Thus, Lubitsch successfully treads the thin line between grotesque caricature and satire.[6]

Lubitsch's dramas of 1918 and early 1919 also tended to stick to the old German norm, using broad, pantomimic acting, exemplified by Pola Negri's sweeping gestures and exaggerated postures in Die Augen der Mumie Mâ (Fig. 5.15).

There is a second impulse in Lubitsch's direction of actors. It was roughly around the time of Madame Dubarry in 1919, that he began to move toward the use of more facial expressions and greater subtlety. One would expect to find further evidence of this shift in Rausch, a *Kammerspiel* (that is, an intimate chamber drama) starring Asta Nielsen. Nielsen, Germany's greatest film actress during the 1910s, was unsurpassed in her ability to convey emotions through posture and gesture, though her face was extremely expressive as well. Nielsen did not work repeatedly with Lubitsch, as most of his other starring actors did, and her performance in this serious drama presumably was quite different from the more bumptious performances of his regular leading ladies. Unfortunately RAUSCH is lost, and Nielsen's brief description of working with Lubitsch is fairly unspecific. Still, it is worth quoting as one of the rare comments on Lubitsch's work with his German actors.

After noting that she had been upset with the many changes Lubitsch and co-scenarist Hans Kräly had made in Strindberg's play, she continues:

> Despite all disputes over the scenario, it was a happy collaboration with Lubitsch. His outstanding abilities as a director were completely obvious to me. With a sure instinct he brought the situations to a clear zenith, and he had a sympathy for the actors; he never struck a wrong note in that. He possessed every degree of artistic comprehension of technique – one could also say: the technical comprehension of the artistic – that constitutes a truly good film director's real talent.[7]

The move toward greater emphasis on facial expression probably resulted in part from Lubitsch's increasing use of editing, which, as we have seen, becomes very apparent by the time of SUMURUN. The emphasis on facial expression would be further encouraged by his move to Hollywood and his increased focus on sophisticated romantic comedy.

Despite working with talented actors like Emil Jannings, Paul Wegener, and Harry Liedtke, Lubitsch usually centered his films around actresses such as Ossi Oswalda, Pola Negri, and Henny Porten. Oswalda's mobile face and energy suited her to portray mischievous, imperious young ladies; so stable was her persona that she often played a character named Ossi, although each was supposed to be a different person. French critics Eithne and Jean-Loup Bourget have offered a revealing description of Oswalda: "A sharp, blonde gamine, a bit chubby, not especially pretty, but overflowing with the same vitality as Lubitsch himself."[8]

This kind of vitality was common among Lubitsch's main actors of this era – in both the comedies and dramas – and that sets them apart from the more slowly-paced performances typical of contemporary German films. At the beginning of ICH MÖCHTE KEIN MANN SEIN, Ossi's governess has scolded her for smoking. Ossi sticks out her tongue behind the governess's back (Fig. 5.16), then quickly changes to an exaggerated smile when the woman turns around to face her (Fig. 5.17). Even Henny Porten, more mature and well-known for her many dramatic roles for other directors, mugged for Lubitsch. In KOHLHIESELS TÖCHTER, loosely based on *The Taming of the Shrew*, Porten played both daughters, willingly looking dimwitted in the role of the pretty Gretel (Fig. 5.18) and downright homely as the termagant Liesl (Fig. 5.19).

The *New York Times* review of MADAME DUBARRY when it played in the United States suggests the indifference to glamor shared by Lubitsch's actresses. Praising Negri, the reviewer specified: "It is not her physical beauty that wins for her. She is lovely in many scenes, it is true, but some of her features are not beautiful, and she makes no apparent effort to pose becomingly without regard to the meaning of her performance. She is expressive. That is her charm."[9] The intensity of Negri's performances in her German films was noticeably damped down after she moved to Hollywood, where her glamorous costumes and exotic European beauty became part of her image.

Biographer Scott Eyman suggests that it was Lubitsch's work with talented actors that led to his blossoming as a director: "Negri's own sense of passionate commitment to craft was transferred to her director; as Lubitsch would later write, 'after making my first dramatic film with Pola Negri and Jannings [DIE AUGEN DER MUMIE MÂ], I completely lost interest in being an actor.'" As the star of his own comedies, Eyman argues convincingly, Lubitsch had primarily used the camera to present his own performances. In directing others, "Lubitsch's concentration began to be focused on the settings, the camera, the ensemble."[10] Although Lubitsch made one additional short comic feature, MEYER AUS BERLIN, his last role on the screen was more ambitious, as the tragicomic clown in the Arabian-Nights fantasy SUMURUN.

The latter film is of interest because it contains Lubitsch's only surviving serious role. Although he had played small parts in Max Reinhardt's famous production of the play SUMURUN, there is no evidence that he ever – as is sometimes claimed – played the hunchbacked clown.[11] Possibly he understudied for this role or is here imitating another stage actor's performance. At any rate, his acting is distinctly theatrical. In the scene where he realizes that the Dancer will never love him, he emotes at length, using broad gestures and a face twisted into a tragic mask (Fig. 5.20) – a technique he employs in closer framings as well as in long shots. The result may have influenced his approach to acting thereafter. According to Horak, Lubitsch had some reservations about SUMURUN: "His own performance as the hunchback, especially Lubitsch thought overacted, even though he received a standing ovation at the Berlin premiere. Lubitsch vowed never again to stand in front of the camera."[12]

SUMURUN was released in America as ONE ARABIAN NIGHT in 1921, and, despite its staginess, Lubitsch's performance won enthusiastic praise. "To the tragic figure of the hunchback," wrote the *New York Times* reviewer, "he gives that personal definiteness which so many screen figures lack, and the intensity of his acting seems to represent the real feeling of his overwrought character rather than the frantic effort of a so-called actor to act."[13] *Variety* was even more enthusiastic: "In this picture he displays the fact that he is just as great an actor as he is a director and his characterization of the Hunchback is one that American character players can well study."[14]

It is difficult to reconcile these paeans with Lubitsch's acting in the film, so different is it from the Hollywood norms of the era. Perhaps the reviewers were still dazzled by the director's sudden rise to the status of the greatest Eu-

ropean director in the wake of MADAME DUBARRY a year earlier. Or perhaps reviewers were tacitly comparing Lubitsch's acting technique with that of Lon
Chaney, who was just rising to fame as a character actor adept at eccentric roles
involving heavy make-up.

Pantomimic acting remained part of Lubitsch's style until near the end of
his German period. Perhaps because of its much larger budget and enormous
sets, the spectacle DAS WEIB DES PHARAO (at least in the portions that survive)
draws almost entirely on broad gestures. Lubitsch largely abandoned this
style for his Hollywood films, though the trailer for the otherwise lost movie
THE PATRIOT hints that Jannings may have revived it for his performance in the
film – albeit he was depicting an insane character.

Alongside such pantomimic acting, one can also see Lubitsch's growing
impulse toward facial expression and occasionally greater restraint. Watching
CARMEN and MADAME DUBARRY side by side, for example, one notices the
changes made in less than a year. An increased dependence on editing helped
to convey character thoughts and reactions. In the scene where Louis XV first
sees Jeanne sitting nearby on the grounds of his palace, the action extends over
shots of the royal entourage and of Jeanne, as she is seen by Louis in a series of
eyeline matches; all Jannings needs to do is smile and look offscreen in a number of shots, and his attraction to her is conveyed without any need for gestures (Fig. 4.50). As we noted in the previous chapter, however, a number of
cuts in this scene cross the axis of action (a continuity convention not familiar
to German filmmakers at this point), creating some confusion about where
Jeanne is in relation to Louis's group. In Hollywood, Lubitsch would hone his
editing until every cut maintained screen direction. More precise eyeline
matching remained one crucial means for conveying information without resorting to intertitles or broad gestures.

By 1922, Lubitsch had seen enough American films to begin adopting the
basics of continuity practice. The few surviving fragments of Lubitsch's last
German film, the melodrama DIE FLAMME, indicate his growing familiarity
with Hollywood-style editing and its use of glances and facial expressions in
building performances. In one scene, Yvette, played by Negri, is dining with
Adolphe, a naive young man who is attracted to her, and Adolphe's older,
more worldly cousin, Raoul. Aside from lifting drinks, the actors' hands do little, and the faces carry the action. In a medium two-shot (Fig. 5.21), Adolphe
looks happily off left at Raoul, followed by a dialogue title, "Did I say too
much to you about Yvette?" A reverse shot of Raoul follows, as he looks know-
ingly rightward at Yvette and responds (Fig. 5.22); a second dialogue title says,
"Much too little." A closer framing just of Yvette follows, with her looking
down and then up and off left at Raoul, worried (Fig. 5.23). Given the state of
the print, it is not clear whether she is worried that Raoul will reveal some-

thing about her shady past or is simply indignant about his leering familiarity; in either case, this and the subsequent action of the scene are conveyed largely by glances, with eyelines correctly matched.

One clue to Lubitsch's technique in eliciting performances from his casts comes from the many published descriptions of how he would mime all the roles himself in explaining them to the actors. An early instance of this appeared in a fan magazine article by a writer who visited the set of DIE FLAMME. The reporter gave a brief but vivid description of how Lubitsch showed the performers what he wanted:

> He bounds among the players to act a 'bit' for a little girl playing a *cocotte*. He is a very funny coquette, but he knows the business, every glance, every wink, every instinctive gesture of the flirt … Then off again on a feverish pace as if he had lost all interest in the affair.[15]

Lubitsch used the same method throughout his Hollywood career, as many more eye-witness accounts testify.

Whether drawing upon a broad, pantomimic style or a more restrained, facial style, Lubitsch sought to tell his stories through visual means whenever possible. Several times he expressed his desire to minimize the use of inter-titles. In 1920, he discussed how films could be kitsch, entertainment, or art, depending on the treatment. Films can be like poetry if their scripts are carefully written: "Film poetry, as I conceive it, should be written neither in a naturalistic nor in an expressionistic style, but it must be composed in images, that is, the treatment must be done in such a way that each image advances the dramatic structure without explanation by intertitles."[16]

Historians usually associate the impulse toward titleless narrative film with the best-known German scenarist of the 1920s, Carl Mayer, who largely accomplished this ideal in four famous examples: SCHERBEN (1921), HINTERTREPPE (1921), SYLVESTER (1923), and DER LETZTE MANN (1924).[17] Lubitsch's 1920 comments on the subject reflect the fact that during the postwar years there was a more general call by critics for "film poetry" that could tell stories in a purely visual way. We shall hear again of this goal and examine Lubitsch's increasingly sophisticated ways of achieving it in his Hollywood films. Lubitsch never went as far as Mayer in eliminating all titles, but he tried his best to avoid them whenever the point could be made with some visual touch – and that often involved bits of business for the actors.

Lubitsch's Hollywood Features

Lubitsch's first Hollywood feature, ROSITA, resembles his German epic films in some ways. It is a light costume drama with large sets and crowd scenes. The plot, reminiscent of both MADAME DUBARRY and SUMURUN, involves a street performer who attracts the eye of a philandering king – though in this case the film ends happily as the queen helps thwart her husband's plan to have Rosita's lover executed. The protagonist would seem to be a Pola Negri role, but she was played in quite a different fashion by Mary Pickford. Clearly she was not about to incorporate broad or grotesque gestures into her performance, and in the scenes of her singing and dancing in the street she looks pretty and charming; she does not reach for the sultry exoticism of Negri (Fig. 5.24). Indeed, even sympathetic reviewers widely remarked on her physical implausibility as a Spanish street dancer, a disparity made all the more apparent by the coincidental premiere of THE SPANISH DANCER only a month later. This Paramount film starred Negri in a similar role and contained parallel plot elements, facts not overlooked by reviewers.

Pickford's performance in ROSITA combines her bubbly persona from earlier films with an attempt at greater depth and maturity. Despite the king's blandishments, her virtue never seems in real danger; her scenes with him combine naiveté and mischievousness. Later, when her lover is arrested and then apparently executed, she displays greater seriousness and even goes briefly mad until she learns that he has survived. The range of emotions she was called upon to display drew praise from critics. Some suggested that ROSITA marked a step upward for Pickford as a serious actress. *Variety*'s enthusiastic review kept returning to Pickford's performance before referring to her director:

> Enter Mary Pickford, actress, as Rosita in a screen production of the same name directed by Ernst Lubitsch. A Mary Pickford greater than at any time in her screen career ...
>
> In "Rosita" she tops the splendid work of "Stella Maris" the greatest picture she ever made until the current feature ...
>
> Here is Mary Pickford in a mad scene that rivals anything that has been done on either stage or screen by the greatest of actresses ...
>
> "Rosita" is going to go down into screen history as the picture that made Mary Pickford a real actress or at least revealed her as one ...
>
> To Lubitsch full credit must be given. He seemingly inspired his cast and compelled them to give greater performances most people thought beyond them [sic].[18]

From the start of his Hollywood career, Lubitsch was given much credit as an inspired director of actors, and that reputation continued to grow throughout the 1920s.

Rosita affords us another glimpse of Lubitsch's distinctive method of directing his actors. Robert Florey, then an historical consultant and assistant to Pickford and Fairbanks, published a brief memoir of the production based on his on-set notes. He described a scene shot on the second day of the production, in which Rosita was trying to flirt with her prison guard in an attempt to escape: "Ernst Lubitsch mimed all this action, at first playing the role of the jailor, then that of Mary. All eyes were fixed on Lubitsch. What a superb actor! Mary Pickford herself was impressed by his pantomime and his advice; at that moment I would not have hesitated to declare Lubitsch the greatest director in the world!"[19]

Other actors who worked with Lubitsch later in his career recalled that he acted out each scene in detail and expected them to copy him closely. Many publicity photographs show him doing so, though these are all posed for the still camera. The photo that seems most closely to reflect Lubitsch's actual behavior on the set is for Rosita (Fig. 5.25). The scene is lit exactly as is the shot of this action in the film (Fig. 5.26), so much so that the illumination flatters the actors but leaves most of Lubitsch's face in shadow. Hence it was probably taken during Lubitsch's actual instructions to the actors. Florey has described Lubitsch directing this shot: "Lubitsch mimed the two roles with great finesse, indicating to the artists what he wanted; his astonishing agility revealed a man of the theater."[20]

Lubitsch planned all the performances during each film's preparation stages. Patsy Ruth Miller, who played the heroine of So This Is Paris, recalled his working methods: "The whole film was visualized in his head, so he wasn't very flexible. He didn't want you going off the beaten track with a gesture if it wasn't what he had in mind."[21] Ali Hubert, who did the costumes for The Patriot, described Lubitsch directing a scene through mime:

> Lubitsch jumps down from the filming platform in order to play vividly for Emil Jannings his part of the scene with Florence Vidor. Suggestively, with affecting gestures, he emphasizes precisely how the insane Tsar courts the completely terrified Countess Ostermann.[22]

Lest one assume that Lubitsch demanded actors to copy him exactly, here is Peter Bogdanovich's account of what Jack Benny later said about working on To Be or Not To Be (1942):

> Jack Benny told me that Lubitsch would act out in detail exactly how he wanted everything done. I asked how he was. "Well," said Jack, "it was a little *broad*, but you

got the *idea*." The comedian explained that Lubitsch knew Benny would translate the direction into his own manner and that this would make it work.[23]

Clearly, though, spontaneity was not a goal for Lubitsch – perfection was, and he was the sort of director to insist on numerous retakes. Based on interviews, Scott Eyman describes this process for the silent period. In relation to Irene Rich's performance during the racetrack scene in LADY WINDERMERE'S FAN, he writes:

> One observer noticed that most directors would have directed Rich through her close-ups by saying something like "You are watching the races – you turn and watch the people – smile. Good heavens? It's your own daughter – turn away."
> But Lubitsch talked Rich through the scene up to the point where she was able to see her daughter. "Now!" he said, and snapped his fingers, causing Rich to stiffen her body. The close-up took nine takes before Lubitsch was satisfied.

Another description touches on Lubitsch's famous love of doors for dramatic purposes:

> For the actors of THE MARRIAGE CIRCLE, used to the hurry-up-and-print-it regimen favored by Jack Warner, Lubitsch was something entirely different; the director found that he had to work his actors harder to get the results he needed. "He made me do simple scenes," complained Marie Prevost, "just coming in and out of rooms fifteen or twenty times. At first it seemed as though there wasn't any sense to it at all. Then it began to dawn upon me what the art of acting was all about, and it seemed intolerably and impossibly difficult. Then I began to see it as he saw it ... He deals in subtleties that I never dreamed of before.[24]

As we shall see, the many actors who were able to meet Lubitsch's demands were rewarded with high praise in reviews.

After ROSITA, Lubitsch moved to Warner Bros. for THE MARRIAGE CIRCLE, which reflects a distinct change in his direction of actors. Historians have usually assumed that the film was influenced by Chaplin's A WOMAN OF PARIS. Chaplin's film premiered in Los Angeles on September 26, 1923, and Lubitsch shot THE MARRIAGE CIRCLE during September and October of that year (the latter premiered on February 3, 1924). Given this sequence of events, Lubitsch would have to have seen Chaplin's film before its release. Unfortunately I have found no smoking-gun memorandum proving that Lubitsch attended a private screening, but very likely he did. United Artists was quite a small operation, with Chaplin, Fairbanks, and Pickford forming a tight group in Los Angeles, and Griffith laboring away on AMERICA in isolation in upstate New York. The firm also released very few films. O'Brien, legal counsel for United Artists, summed up the situation to Pickford and Fairbanks in a letter written October 17, 1923, describing a recent meeting:

Mr. Abrams then stated that the corporation had a very serious problem ahead of it on account of lack of product. That the only pictures he had at present were the pictures of last year, ROSITA and A WOMAN OF PARIS, and the pictures of the Associated Authors; that Douglas would, no doubt, road show his THIEF OF BAGDAD, and Mr. Griffith would, no doubt, road show the big picture he is now making, and that the corporation couldn't possibly live on the returns of the old pictures and those two pictures for the period of a year.

This is a serious matter and ought to be considered immediately and some remedy sought rather than allow ourselves to get in a bad financial condition in the spring time. It may be that Charlie would come through with a quick picture, and that Mary will finish DOROTHY VERNON OF HADDON HALL in time for the United Artists to market it in the early winter. It would be welcomed news to all concerned.[25]

Aside from providing further evidence of the financial difficulties that led Lubitsch to leave United Artists, O'Brien's comments vividly show that in terms of scheduling, Lubitsch's and Chaplin's 1923 films were running parallel. Both men began editing in June. The New York premieres were undoubtedly spaced a month apart (September 3 for ROSITA, October 1 for A WOMAN OF PARIS) so that they would not compete with each other. Given the paucity of activity at United Artists, it would seem odd if Lubitsch did not see some version of A WOMAN OF PARIS that summer – the very time he would have been planning THE MARRIAGE CIRCLE.

Many reviewers compared the two films. They praised Adolphe Menjou's performance in A WOMAN OF PARIS for its restraint and subtlety. One memorable scene shows Menjou, as the heroine's lover casually playing his miniature saxophone while Marie tries to break off their affair (Fig. 5.27). Lubitsch chose Menjou for THE MARRIAGE CIRCLE; he was the only major cast member who was not a regular Warners player. And Lubitsch's admiration for Chaplin is certainly well-known. In 1926, a snobbish journalist asked Lubitsch why he was "satisfied to direct light comedy when you might do another 'Passion'?" Lubitsch cited Molière and Chaplin as great comic artists, but the interviewer dismissed Chaplin as "hardly to be compared with Molière." Lubitsch, clearly incensed, replied, "THE WOMAN OF PARIS – THE WOMAN OF PARIS – a masterpiece – such genius – such genius." After a few more exchanges, Lubitsch dismissed his interlocutor with a well-deserved "Oh, let me alone" – which the reporter blithely quoted along with all the rest in his article![26]

In his memoirs, Menjou recorded some revealing differences between Chaplin's and Lubitsch's direction of actors. He recalled learning how to give a nuanced performance in A WOMAN OF PARIS:

Within a few days I realized that I was going to learn more about acting from Chaplin than I had ever learned from any director. He had one wonderful, unforgettable
line that he kept repeating over and over throughout the picture. "Don't sell it!" he
would say. "Remember, they're peeking at you."

It was a colorful and concise way to sum up the difference between the legitimate
stage and the movies – a reminder that in pictures, when one has an important emotion or thought to express, the camera moves up to his face and there he is on the
screen with a head that measures 6 feet from brow to chin. The audience is peeking
at him under a microscope, so he can't start playing to the gallery 200 feet away, because there is no gallery in a movie theater; the audience is sitting in his lap ...

Since then I have never played a scene before a camera without thinking to myself,
"They're peeking at you, don't sock it."

Menjou described how delighted he was to work on THE MARRIAGE CIRCLE,
but evidently he learned much less:

Lubitsch, as a director, had the same regard for realistic and subtle touches as Chaplin, but his methods were entirely different. Lubitsch planned everything very carefully in advance; he knew the content of every scene before he began shooting, and
he acted out every part in rehearsal. I discovered in this picture that all I had to do to
make Lubitsch happy was to step before the camera and mimic every gesture he
gave me.[27]

Again, the suggestion is that Lubitsch acted the roles himself for the performers and expected them to imitate him.

Although all the cast members of THE MARRIAGE CIRCLE received praise in
the reviews, Menjou was particularly singled out: "[Mitzi's] husband, as
played by Menjou, is a work of art. Repressed in style is his work, but with a
touch of the finer little things, such as an arched eyebrow, a smile or a wink
that means volumes."[28] That Lubitsch had achieved his goal of avoiding unnecessary intertitles is suggested by the *Moving Picture World*'s reviewer: "It is
an excellent example of finely handled pantomime; there is minimum of subti-
tles, but few are needed, for the situations are so deftly handled as to render
them unnecessary."[29] Menjou played a supporting role in Lubitsch's next feature, FORBIDDEN
PARADISE, as well, and was praised in similar terms:

Strikingly effective is the performance of Adolphe Menjou. Always a good actor, he
displays unusually fine subtlety and finesse in the role of the court chancellor, the
only one who really understands the queen. On his shoulders falls most of the clever
comedy, and he deftly puts it over, many of his biggest points being registered by the
lifting of an eyebrow or an almost imperceptible gesture.[30]

As we shall see, however, there were moments in this film where Menjou's expressions were a trifle more obvious than this reviewer suggests. Perhaps Menjou's reputation for subtlety had already, however, solidified.

As with ROSITA, reviewers credited Lubitsch – probably rightly – with being a great director of actors. Compare the following comments from reviews of some of his mid-1920s films:

> [THE MARRIAGE CIRCLE:] He has inspired his players with vivaciousness, and although all are good usually in their screen work, they are much better under his artistic and astute instruction.[31]
>
> [THE MARRIAGE CIRCLE:] By no means the least of Mr. Lubitsch's accomplishments is his superb handling of his players. Adolphe Menjou equals his performance in "A Woman of Paris," Monte Blue and Marie Prevost in the leading roles and Florence Vidor and Creighton Hale as well measure up to the same standard in characterizations quite different from their usual types. Mr. Lubitsch has brought out to the utmost the abilities of his players.[32]
>
> [FORBIDDEN PARADISE:] In the hands of Lubitsch the acting of Pola Negri, Rod la Roque and Adolphe Menjou was so dazzlingly above, not merely the level of these three sound performers, but so much above the level of all but about ten pictures ever played.[33]
>
> [LADY WINDERMERE'S FAN:] Without disparaging the work of the players themselves, the hand of Mr. Lubitsch is evident in their portrayals.[34]
>
> [LADY WINDERMERE'S FAN:] Irene Rich gives a splendid, striking performance, probably the best work she has ever done, thanks to Lubitsch.[35]
>
> [SO THIS IS PARIS:] As in his previous work, Mr. Lubitsch in this new film proves his ability to handle players. He is able to obtain from them restrained and comprehensive expressions and gestures such as they might never register under another producer. Here Mr. Lubitsch takes his old favorite, Monte Blue, who again inculcates life into a part that might easily have been a dull or mediocre characterization.[36]

Hubert made a similar comment in his 1930 book on Hollywood, including his work with Lubitsch:

> Since with this film [THE MARRIAGE CIRCLE] he immediately advanced Monte Blue and Menjou into the first rank of performers, every actor seeks to become an international star under his direction, which naturally contributes not a little to his popularity in the film world.
>
> Today he has the first place in Hollywood, as well as the trust of all producers. The best actors compete to be able to prove themselves on the screen under his direction.[37]

Certainly at Warner Bros. Lubitsch worked with contract players who outdid themselves for him. Only once or twice did he have the chance to work with top-rank stars, and then it was primarily with the up-and-coming Ronald Colman in LADY WINDERMERE'S FAN. (Menjou was also still emerging as a star when Lubitsch cast him in THE MARRIAGE CIRCLE, and no doubt it was one of the roles that set his persona.)

That same year, 1924, Lubitsch again expressed his opinion about how to use acting to minimize the need for intertitles, stressing that a director must collaborate with the scenarist (an approach to pre-production common in Germany) in planning all the "little pieces of business." Of the shooting phase he wrote:

> Then comes the hardest task of the director: to show the actors how to portray these characters on the screen. The trouble with many of the actors today is that they have just a small number of stock gestures and set facial expressions which they repeat over and over again, no matter what the situation really calls for.[38]

The performances in THE MARRIAGE CIRCLE – particularly Menjou's – suggest that Lubitsch was consciously experimenting with how far he could push the use of gestures and tiny facial expressions to express a whole series of a character's thoughts with a minimum of intertitles. The most extreme example comes in the scene when Prof. Stock (played by Menjou) comes home and discovers Dr. Braun with his wife Mitzi. Braun leaves, and Mitzi notices that the pistol she has used to pretend she was going to commit suicide is lying on the floor. To prevent Stock's noticing it, Mitzi crosses to where he is standing in the door, embraces him, and says she wants to make love. Given that the two are estranged and Stock believes Mitzi is having an affair with Braun, he initially reacts with astonishment (Fig. 5.28). He goes through an internal debate for some time, decides Mitzi is sincere, and tenderly pats her shoulder. This shot lasts roughly forty seconds in an era in which the average shot length was five seconds. During the series of glances that Stock casts down at Mitzi and then offscreen in abstracted thought, Marie Prevost, playing Mitzi, remains absolutely still. Lubitsch has also focused attention on Menjou's performance by leaving the door nearly blank, without the panelling present on the film's other doors.

So how did he guide his actors to give performances that gained them so much praise? One answer might lie in Lubitsch's practice of miming all the roles himself. Presumably if the actors successfully imitated him, they would be crafted into an ensemble sharing a unified style. Menjou's forty-second shot in THE MARRIAGE CIRCLE was perhaps a bit too obviously virtuoso (and Prevost's immobility too apparent) to be wholly successful. It makes his acting stand apart from that of the other cast members. Certainly Lubitsch never tried such an extended moment of reflection again. Yet, from this film on, the acting in his American features is characterized by a slower pace than in most of his

German films. The actors have time to register the nuances of their reactions and interactions.

Moreover, Lubitsch's growing mastery of the subtleties of continuity editing allowed him to create a play of eyeline directions, offscreen glances, and other techniques to build performances without the need for sustained facial play within any one shot – perhaps one reason that some actors did their best work under his direction. There are famous examples, such as the opening scene of THE MARRIAGE CIRCLE, where Stock's point-of-view glances into two dresser drawers – his own nearly empty, his wife's stuffed with stockings – quickly sums up the state of their marriage. Another occurs in LADY WINDERMERE'S FAN, where Lady Windermere reacts in shock (Fig. 5.29) when she thinks she sees Mrs. Erlynne's hand being kissed by her husband (Fig. 5.30); a 180° cut reveals to the audience what she cannot see, that Mrs. Erlynne's companion is really an elderly bachelor (Fig. 5.31).

But the technique is also employed in more ordinary scenes. Take a brief example from THREE WOMEN. A young woman is holding a birthday party, and her shy suitor takes her outside to give her his present. As she sits on a bench waiting with her eyes closed, a cut-in to a medium shot shows the young man searching his pockets, then glancing offscreen right, toward the house (Fig. 5.32). There is a cut to his coat – in the pocket of which he has left the present – lying on a chair inside (Fig. 5.33). A medium long shot of the two shows her still waiting expectantly (Fig. 5.34), while he hurries out right toward the house. In medium close-up, the woman opens her eyes in puzzlement at the delay (Fig. 5.35), then glances off right toward the house, followed by her point-of-view long shot of her suitor racing toward the house (Fig. 5.36). His glance and the cutaway to the coat inform us of why he cannot give her the present, and her surprised look conveys her incomprehension about why he has left her so abruptly. This scene leads immediately to her separation from the young man and subsequent marriage to a cad, so the delay in his handing the present over has had major consequences. Editing around eyelines was universal in Hollywood films, of course, but in his quest to minimize intertitles, Lubitsch found ways to maximize its power and subtlety.

One contemporary reviewer praised THREE WOMEN in a way that again stresses the paucity of intertitles, although he suggests that Lubitsch may have occasionally overdone it:

> An outstanding feature of this photoplay is the sparing manner in which subtitles are employed. It has fewer captions than any other film we have seen which had subtitles at all. Mr. Lubitsch's able direction has caused the actions and expressions of the players to be readily understood, thus rendering subtitles unnecessary for long stretches ...

> The court room scene is a bit feeble, and the idea of the foreman giving the verdict by shaking his head, so that Mr. Lubitsch would not have to insert a subtitle, is a little strained.[39]

This comment also shows that at least some reviewers were aware of Lubitsch's attempts to minimize inter-titles.

All this is not to suggest that Lubitsch's films of this period do not contain examples of broad acting. Even that master of subtlety, Adolphe Menjou, was capable of smiling suggestively and rolling his eyes in response to a risqué situation in FORBIDDEN PARADISE (Figs. 5.37 and 5.38). (The expression is similar to his knowing smirk upon seeing the gigolo in the restaurant scene of A WOMAN OF PARIS, though there he does not roll his eyes.) Moreover, the films vary in their acting styles. While LADY WINDERMERE'S FAN emphasizes subtlety and dignified comedy in a basically dramatic narrative, SO THIS IS PARIS is closer to bedroom farce and is played appropriately. When the protagonist meets an old lover, the two sit and begin to reminisce delightedly (Fig. 5.39). She begins to pantomime something that happened in the past (Fig. 5.40), to which he reacts by putting his fist to his mouth in an effort to recall the event (Fig. 5.41). Finally he does, and the pair explode in guffaws (Fig. 5.42).

The one exception to Lubitsch's masterful guiding of actors during this period was THE STUDENT PRINCE IN OLD HEIDELBERG. This is a more charming film than one might expect, given the fact that its source is an old-fashioned play. Jean Hersholt's performance as Prince Karl Heinrich's tutor was widely praised and nominated for the first Academy Award for best supporting actor. The two leads, however, proved less satisfactory. Lubitsch's assistant and editor, Andrew Marton, recalled in an interview the problems with the first big love scene between Prince Karl and the beer-hall waitress Kathi:

> It was a scene that Lubitsch still hated after he re-did it. There were other problems with the meadow scene besides the set – the chemistry was not the way Lubitsch imagined it. He never thought that Ramon Novarro or Norma Shearer was the right casting for the film, but the studio insisted and he was stuck with them. Lubitsch did marvelously with them, actually, but not to his exacting standards.[40]

Shearer in particular is not up to her role, as is apparent in her first appearance in the film. She meets Karl as he arrives at the inn where she works (Fig. 5.43). The camera re-frames left as she walks around Karl, supposedly staring at him in naive admiration (Fig. 5.44); unfortunately her gaze conveys something closer to fascinated lust.

It seems fairly obvious that in some of their scenes together, Lubitsch achieved a better result by giving the pair simple instructions about facial expressions and directions for glances, orchestrating these so that Kathi's movements seem to echo Karl's. In the later love scene in the boat, the two are care-free and laughing until Karl remembers that they must soon part. He becomes glum while Kathi keeps on smiling (Fig. 5.45). Her smile fades and the two stare sadly away from each other (Fig. 5.46). Kathi tries to revive the cheerful mood by smiling tentatively (Fig. 5.47), before giving up and turning away (Fig. 5.48). Reviewers, generally so kind to Lubitsch's actors, were less pleased with Shearer. The *Moving Picture World*'s reviewer opined that she was mis-cast, and Mordaunt Hall blamed her rather than Lubitsch for the problem:

> Mr. Novarro is natural and earnest, but he is a little too Latin in appearance for the role. Norma Shearer is attractive as Kathi. She, however, does not seem to put her soul into the part. She, too, acts well but, like Mr. Novarro, she does not respond, as other players have done, to Mr. Lubitsch's direction. The ablest acting in this piece of work is done by Jean Hersholt as Dr. Guttner [sic] and Gustav von Seyffertitz as the King. Their efforts in all their scenes reveal their sensitivity to the direction.[41]

One can only hope that Lubitsch's reunion with Jannings for THE PATRIOT was a more congenial experience.

Over the past four chapters, I have traced how Lubitsch went from being a skillful practitioner of the general "rough continuity" of the European cinema of the 1910s, with its diffuse lighting, aggressive sets, and pantomimic acting to being one of the great masters of 1920s Hollywood style. Few of Lubitsch's fellow countrymen ever came to Hollywood. Historians tend to exaggerate the supposed exodus of talent from Germany, but although prominent directors like Paul Leni and Murnau departed, many more, like Karl Grune, Wilhelm Thiele, and Erich Schönfelder, stayed. Through the work of such filmmakers, the classical cinema's influence took hold within German filmmaking. In the next chapter, I will show that Expressionism and *Neue Sachlichkeit* were minor strains of distinctly German cinema within a prolific national industry that increasingly imitated its successful American rival.

6 Mutual Influences

Equipping for Influence: The Modernization of German Studios

In the mid-1920s, Robert Florey offered some advice to French film producers wanting to compete with the Americans. His suggestions, pertinent to other national film industries as well, usefully summarize the beliefs widely held within the German film industry of 1921 and after:

> It would seem necessary, for a start, to install some good, large studios equipped with all the modern improvements, and above all lights, indispensable lights. In these same studios there would need to be built sets which do not have the feel of sets, props which do not make the public laugh, in short everything which contributes to producing a normal film – so normal that one would forget its nationality. Because of this, it becomes international. It can show on all the screens of the world, so that all audiences can understand it as they understand simple, normal American films, but properly, clearly, adequately staged, with light, a great deal of light, and performed by actors trained for the cinema and who have not had to reach the screen after remaining on the stage for 35 years.[1]

Florey assumes "normal" films to be classical films, as made in Hollywood. They would have realistic-looking sets, lights directed into the scene from multiple points, cinematic acting, and above all comprehensibility ("*simple, normal American films*").

I have argued that Lubitsch was simply the first and best of the German directors of popular cinema to integrate Hollywood influences into his films. We have seen that Lang and Murnau adapted aspects of continuity editing in their Expressionist films, but Lubitsch was earliest, I believe, to adopt the combination of techniques that constituted classical filmmaking. On a technical level, particularly in regard to lighting, he was able to do so because he had access to the American-style facilities of the EFA studio. The technical journals of the day suggest that other filmmakers would have liked to have made films in the new Hollywood style, but they were hampered by a lack of facilities. Nevertheless, as more dark studios were built and equipped with a variety of lamps, three-point lighting replaced the diffused sunlight and glaring, frontal arclight of the postwar years. Continuity "rules" of editing were less easy to assimilate, since the principle of maintaining constant screen direction would not be obvious when viewing a film; like Lubitsch, directors would learn cutting techniques more gradually. Nevertheless, by 1925, films that looked very much like their Hollywood counterparts were common, probably even dominant, in Germany. Even the vaunted German-style set design, the one aspect of the country's cinema that was internationally praised, began to be less conspicuous as the decade wore on. Large, eye-catching, and decidedly German sets lingered on, but by the second half of the decade, inconspicuous, realistic spaces ceded the attention almost entirely to the actors and to verisimilitude.

It is no coincidence, as I have suggested, that Expressionism declined in these very years. Expressionism was in many ways an exact opposite of classical style. It subordinated the actors' movements to the very conspicuous space surrounding them. It relied on simple, frontal framing to allow the sets to create pictorial compositions. It generally encouraged flat, frontal lighting, since the compositional elements were usually contained within the shapes and surfaces of the sets. It used analytical editing primarily to eliminate the sets and concentrate the spectator's attention on the actors for brief periods during which the story was being advanced. The actors themselves often moved in exaggerated, theatrical ways that were more reminiscent of primitive pantomime than of the subtle flow of changing facial expressions developed in Hollywood during the 1910s. As German cinema became more Americanized, films tended to look simpler and sleeker, to move at a faster rate as a result of increased analytical editing, and to tell more straightforward, comprehensible stories. Erich Schönfelder's charming 1926 Lilian Harvey comedy, VATER WERDEN IST NICHT SCHWER (IT'S EASY TO BECOME A FATHER) far better typifies Germany's output that year than does Murnau's FAUST, one of the last gasps of the Expressionist movement.

Even before the import ban was lifted, people in the German film industry were interested in and aware of developments in Hollywood. In 1920, the main trade paper, the *Lichtbildbühne*, ran a series of articles, "From the American Film Industry." The author described how dark studios, lit entirely with mercury-vapor and arc lamps, were common in Hollywood. Unlike in the German studios, the arcs could be controlled from a single panel, permitting complex lighting effects. Weinert and Jupiters had to be directly controlled by individual technicians, and hence such effects were impossible in Germany. The 150-amp sunlight arcs of American manufacture were far brighter than any German spotlight available at the time.[2] In the same year, the American Consul in Berlin reported that German lighting facilities were poor by Hollywood standards, though they were improving. Some German glass studios had supplemental electric lighting, and the summer sun was adequate for filmmaking – though companies would also go on location to the Mediterranean to take advantage of the brighter light, as well as fresh scenery.[3]

Soon, however, the German move toward building dark studios or converting old glass-sided ones to eliminate sunlight began. In 1922, a huge converted zeppelin hangar was opened as the Staaken film studio, and it was rented out mostly for films requiring large sets. Parts of METROPOLIS were later shot there. Staaken was hailed as the first German studio capable of competing with Hollywood in terms of its lighting outfit. It had a large curved cyclorama and many lamps, which could be moved in response to a director issuing orders via telephone.[4]

One historical account credited a street scene in Lang's DR. MABUSE DER SPIELER (1922), filmed in the Jofa studio, as the first to shoot a scene in an exterior setting in a dark studio. In 1923, another large Berlin company, Terra, outfitted its glass studio with transformers and lighting equipment that would help it meet "the high demands of modern direction." In 1927, a British industry observer visited Ufa's new dark studio and commented that the glass in the older Ufa buildings had been painted dark blue – a common expedient in Hollywood and elsewhere to create a dark studio at minimal expense.[5]

During these same years, American-style technology was making its way into the German industry. In 1922, Jupiter brought out its own version of the intense sunlight arc spot, making shooting night-for-night exteriors outdoors much more feasible. (We have seen sunlight arcs, probably of American manufacture, used for this purpose in DAS WEIB DES PHARAO; see Fig. 2.82). Also in 1922, the same company began marketing a brighter twelve-lamp arc unit. Erich Pommer later described his first trip to America in 1924: "I went back, telling the technicians over there that film lights used in the United States were the best that I had ever seen. Incidentally, I took with me one of every kind of light I had found in the United States."[6]

Although camera design had less impact on the types of stylistic devices I am examining in this book, German interest in American technology in general can be seen again in their interest in precision-made all-metal cameras like the Bell & Howell and Mitchell models. Up to this point, German filming had been done with the standard European wooden box-style cameras made by Debrie, Ernemann, and other firms. In 1921, the Deutschen Kinotechnischen Gesellschaft hosted a demonstration of the Bell & Howell, which was found to have several features not available on European models. The camera itself may well have been one of those used by Lubitsch on DAS WEIB DES PHARAO. Growing inflation made it difficult to import equipment, but by 1922 Bell & Howells were in occasional use in German studios.[7] Production shots show Lang filming METROPOLIS with Bell & Howells. Similarly, when American cinematographer Charles Rosher toured Germany in 1924, he carried with him the prototype Mitchell camera that he had acquired in 1920 – the same camera he had used when filming ROSITA for Lubitsch the year before. This and other pieces of equipment were examined with great interest by the cinematographers and technicians he met, including Lubitsch's previous cinematographer,

Theodor Sparkuhl, the great Fritz Arno Wagner - and Ufa's technical director, Otto Ostermayr, who immediately placed an order for ten thousand dollars' worth of Mitchell equipment.[8]

German Cinema Goes Hollywood

By the mid-1920s, the effects of changing technologies and stylistic practices were evident in most ordinary German films. Since the same examples will often serve to display the various developments in lighting, set design, editing, and acting, I shall not review each area of technique separately. Instead, I shall move chronologically through a number of films representative of the standard, and in some cases high-budget, German studio product.

Karl Grune's EIFERSUCHT (1925) was a fairly large star vehicle for Werner Krauss and Lya de Putti. Essentially a melodramatic *Kammerspiel*, it contains three-point lighting in most scenes (Fig. 6.1), shot/reverse-shot conversations (Figs. 6.2 and 6.3), and a large street set which, while Germanic in its style, was built in a dark studio and lit artificially (Fig. 6.4). The interior sets are simple and unobtrusive, and the acting is relatively restrained, with emotions being conveyed to a large extent through expressions and eyelines across a series of analytical shots. Though not a famous auteur, Grune was one of the prominent directors of the period, known best today for DIE STRASSE. One might expect him to have grasped Hollywood principles better than most. Yet more ordinary films of the mid-1920s demonstrate repeatedly that German filmmakers not only understood analytical editing and, in most cases, the 180-degree rule, but that they even quickly adopted the relatively new Hollywood practice of placing the shoulder or head of the listening figure in the side foreground of shot/reverse shots, such as in these typical examples: from EINE ANSTÄNDIGE FRAU (1925; Figs. 6.5 and 6.6), DIE LETZTE DROSCHKE VON BERLIN (1926; Figs. 6.7 and 6.8), and DER MANN IM FEUER (1926; Figs. 6.9 and 6.10). All three sets of illustrations also reflect the principle of making settings recede during closer framings of the characters, both through simplicity of design and through the use of subdued fill light on the sets. Despite the darker backgrounds, characters in dark clothing stand out as a result of rim lighting.

Occasionally, as we saw in EIFERSUCHT, an eye-catching set appears in a film, but it tends to be used in a limited way, such as for dramatically emphasizing a major scene. DAS PANZERGEWÖLBE, for example, is a 1926 mystery thriller, and the villains' lair – the armored vault of the title – is represented by a big, strikingly simple set that creates a beautiful composition (Fig. 6.11). The film's other sets, however, are unobtrusive. A closely framed conversation takes place before a nearly neutral wall highlighted with a discreet border well above the playing area (Fig. 6.12). Note also how fill light has been used to soften and minimize the shadows cast by the two actors on the wall. A large beer-hall set is de-emphasized by strong backlighting that focuses attention on the figures (Fig. 6.13). Both the set design and lighting are remarkably similar to a shot from a party scene in DADDY-LONG-LEGS (Fig. 6.14), indicating how much German film style had changed in the five years since the Pickford film was released in Germany.

Not surprisingly, the stylistic traits picked up from Hollywood films remained central to German filmmaking into the later years of the decade. Another Thiele comedy, HURRAH! ICH LEBE!, from 1928 (Fig. 6.15), keeps the lighting more high-key, yet the sets avoid patterned wallpaper, paintings, or other elaborate decoration to draw the eye away from the actors. The small, crisp shadow cast on the wall by the young man's sleeve contrasts considerably with the multiple shadows that we saw falling on the sets in German films of the immediate post-war years. Joe May's 1928 prestige picture for Ufa, HEIM-KEHR, contains over-the-shoulder shot/reverse shot passages (Figs. 6.16 and 6.17) and three-point lighting of figures against simple, functional sets (Fig. 6.18). DIE WUNDERBARE LÜGE DER NINA PETROWNA (1929), another big Ufa production and a star vehicle for Brigitte Helm, features deep, clean sets (Fig. 6.19) and glamour lighting (Fig. 6.20) that make it resemble the star vehicles then being made with Greta Garbo at MGM.

Contemporary Discussions of American-Style Techniques

These influences did not creep into the German cinema unnoticed. Quite the contrary, the industry press contains detailed and specific discussions of film techniques, often explicitly comparing German and American methods.

In the area of lighting, Germans were eager to hear about the new dark studios that had come into use in Hollywood. In late 1921, *Die Kinotechnik* ran an historical summary of the growing use of dark studios in the US since 1910. It was written by the head of a Chicago production company who pointed out the disadvantages of glass-sided studios, which included the heat and the difficulty of creating dark scenes. He concluded by extolling the new American facilities in a way that must have made German filmmakers grit their teeth:

> Such an artificially lit studio is certainly costly in the preparation, but what endless advantages it offers! If, as I hear, the great German companies are merging or working with a capital of over a hundred million, then cost cannot be an obstacle in the homeland to modernizing the workshop in which the commercial product is cre-

ated, in order to make the photography of German cinema so excellent that it can stand up against American competition ...

In our 'Dark Studios' [in English in the original] we photograph better and we produce more cheaply than you in Germany in your glass studios, which we long ago gave up.[9]

By 1928, the Germans had largely accomplished the conversion to dark-studio shooting with artificial lighting based largely on the classical three-point system. One of the most perceptive commentators on the German cinema of the 1920s, Georg Otto Stindt, summarized the move to dark studios in Germany:

The irregularity of actinic sunshine, the considerable cloudiness of Central Europe and the inconvenient variations in temperature on different days and seasons made it impossible to operate studio efficiently. The glass houses soon disappeared, to give way to the newly built, artificially lit studios; the ones still standing were adapted with curtains or blue paint over the panes.[10]

As we have seen, this last technique was a common expedient used for speedy conversions of old studios.

Stindt also editorialized against old-fashioned lighting practice in German films, by which he meant overall, diffuse illumination, especially in cases where it obviously did not come from the ostensible sources within the setting. An illustration of a large dance scene with flat lighting led him to say:

Light comes from everywhere, much light, too much light! From the chandelier, it does not come at all, nor from the wall-candles; all these hang dead as dummies. The purpose of light fixtures is missed; they become lies, inconspicuous decorations.

He claimed that the illumination must be "painted" into the scene – that is, using directional, selective light sources – as was being done in Hollywood.[11] By that point, German filmmakers were well on their way to achieving that ideal.

As we saw in Chapters Two and Three, one primary function of selective lighting in classical Hollywood films was to model the actors more three-dimensionally (and often more glamorously) while allowing the sets to recede by casting dimmer fill light on them. This approach worked in combination with the growing emphasis on simplicity of set design. The Germans were well aware of this and other techniques used in Hollywood to make the sets less distracting. Again, Stindt wrote a careful summary of the different means filmmakers had at their disposal for, as his article's title called it, "the liberation from the background." He used five photos, all from American films, as examples to prove his points. One could emphasize foreground characters by casting patches of bright illumination on them and keeping the set behind in subdued light. Stindt then discusses in some detail how different lens lengths could affect background, with longer lenses tending to keep the actors sharply focused while allowing the planes behind them to go fuzzy. For close-ups he recommended circular filters or mattes, which would concentrate attention on the face and largely eliminate the background. Stindt even takes into consideration how different colors in the sets and costumes would register on film, and he advises using color contrasts to make the figures stand out against the backgrounds. He concludes: "Thus one sees that a whole range of means stands at our disposal for liberating us from the background."[12]

The use of filters and long lenses reflects another Hollywood influence: the "soft style" of cinematography, borrowed from pictorialist still photography of the early Twentieth Century.[13] The soft style, which also used large scrims, smoke, and other techniques gave a slightly glowing, fuzzy look to the image. This style had gradually moved into American cinema from the late 1910s, particularly with D.W. Griffith's Broken Blossoms (1919). German filmmakers picked up on it fairly quickly, and it was referred to by the English term "soft focus," for there was no German term for the concept. One expert (who proposes "Unterschärfe" as a possible term) dated the beginning of the German "fashion" for soft-focus cinematography to 1923.[14] In 1928, Die Filmtechnik ran an article detailing the technical means of achieving soft focus, surveying various sorts of filters and filter-holders, wavy glass plates, and lenses. In particular, the authors discuss the American-made "Rosher-Porträt" lens, a lens invented by Charles Rosher (cinematographer of Rosita) for soft-style close shots of actors. German optical companies also made portrait lenses for this same purpose.[15]

Once again an American influence had worked to the detriment of the Expressionist movement. De-emphasizing the sets obviously defeated one of the strongest tools of the Expressionist filmmaker. Moreover, where Expressionist design aimed at fusing actor and setting into a composition designed to look a certain way on the flat screen, classical sets emphasized volumetric space and separated the actors from their backgrounds. During the mid-1920s set designers and commentators carried on a lengthy debate as to whether designers should act as painters or as architects. This debate apparently was initiated in 1924 by Walther Reimann, one of the designers for Das Cabinet des Dr. Caligari. He argued the painterly position, claiming that the designer should work closely with the director and cinematographer to plan the film's shots as unified visual compositions. Those who took the "architect" position pointed out that most sets were three-dimensional and were actually constructed and hence should be planned as buildings. Studios were increasingly dividing labor, and it was not efficient for the director, cinematographer, and designer to coordinate every shot's composition in advance. So the architect faction gradually edged out the painterly faction, though even when the debate started, flat, eye-catching Expressionist sets were already going out of fashion.

Reimann seems to have blamed American influence for at least part of the opposition to painterly set design. In 1925, the year when Ufa re-released CALIGARI, he wrote in defense of experimentation and adventurousness in filmmaking:

> Every project is perilous for an entertaining and exciting art – and film is one such! Americanism, when violently applied, is perilous for film; seeing everything through the old-fashioned spectacles of "just naturalism" is perilous, and naturally it would be just as perilous now to have an era of "Expressionism" begin all at once. But away in general with all "isms"! – because the most perilous are methods, the only sanctioned recipes, that want to pour dream and reality from a bottle.[16]

Reimann's suggestion (and presumably hope) that a new era of Expressionism might begin was not realized, and instead, "Americanism" dominated mainstream filmmaking at the time of his writing.

One participant in the painter-vs.-architect debate, L. Witlin, favored the view of the designer as architect responded to Reimann, using appeals familiar from the classical cinema. To Reimann's claim that the director, designer, and cinematographer should preplan all the shots together, Witlin replied that they all had separate tasks in a collective: "A great part of the success lies in the division of labor [*Teilung der Arbeit*]." He went on to argue against a "horizontal" approach, by which he meant the flat screen compositions favored by Reimann and the Expressionists, and "vertical" space, by which he meant creating a sense of depth through analytical cut-ins:

> The horizontal development on the surface will dissolve into the vertical – toward depth. Film technique gives us the possibility for close-ups, and this means of expression takes us into the realm of the human soul. Here the filmic art promises us unforeseen possibilities.[17]

Striking a cautiously diplomatic note in regard to the painter-vs.-architect debate, Stindt also referred to the American-style division of labor in relation to sets. The director, he commented in a 1926 article on analytical editing, had become more important because the director has more people working under him: "The director of tomorrow will be satisfied – and he knows why – if he can depend entirely upon his painter-architect."[18]

Reimann's counter-argument was that even in a rationalized, American-style system of production, painterly settings offered advantages. He acknowledged that, "Now, however, when the demands of the times necessitate the greatest economy and most rational utilization of all workers, one must truly be concerned with that." In the face of a star-driven, character-oriented cinema, he argued the minority opinion: "The great experience of a film is certainly only in very few cases the personality of an actor; usually it is due to the interesting handling of a strongly conceived milieu." According to Reimann, an imaginative designer, working closely with the scenarist from the beginning of pre-production, could conceive painterly sets that would be much cheaper to build than the large, solid, three-dimensional décors increasingly favored by the studios.[19] It was a position not likely to gain favor in a studio system increasingly based around editing.

The growing use of analytical editing involved moving the camera forward toward the actors and hence militated in favor of extending the playing space into depth – an actual, three-dimensional depth, not one suggested by painterly touches. Again, Georg Otto Stindt contributed an unusually detailed and insightful discussion of editing to the German technical press. In 1926, he described the results of his studies in the relative lengths of shots in German and American films. Good American films, he noticed, increased the number of shots per reel toward the end. As examples he used THE SIN FLOOD (1922, Goldwyn), where the increase was from 88 shots in an early reel to 103 at the end, and THE KID (1921, Charles Chaplin), which went from 52 to 75. Interestingly, Stindt picked one of the most avant-garde of the Expressionist films, Leopold Jessner's ERDGEIST (1923) as his German counterexample: "In a very unfilmic film, ERDGEIST, by Jessner, the total falls from 86 to 48 scenes at the end. There is certainly no better argument for claim that numbers of shots should increase than ERDGEIST." Stindt also found that the average shot length (nowadays abbreviated ASL) of German films had fallen from twelve seconds in 1921 to seven seconds by 1923-rather a remarkable drop in just two years. The ASL for Hollywood films during this time was roughly five seconds.

In addition to editing rhythm, Stindt had clearly thought carefully about the ease of legibility in relation to shot length. He considered twenty frames (one second) was enough for a close-up of a face, ten frames for a burning rafter, and three (with the middle frame completely blank) for a lightning flash. He cited a quickly cut scene of a circus fire in Rupert Hughes's SOULS FOR SALE (1923): "certainly a frantic tempo, but completely intelligible, completely comprehensible." He advocated a variety of shot lengths: "The individual shots of a film must flow together lightly and spontaneously, tightening and shortening, lingering and rushing, as our thoughts do."[20] It was a description of which any Hollywood editor would approve, but one that seems miles away from the conception of editing that predominated in Germany during the immediate postwar years.

In late 1927, Adolf Kobitzsch published an equally remarkable study of editing which emphasized the necessity for a smooth flow from shot to shot. He pointed out that the changes in the vantage-point and scale of each new shot meant that the spectator had – at least for an instant – to "find his way back," to understand the second image as a continuation of the first. He advocated keeping the center of interest roughly in the same area of the screen in the second shot. If there was a movement matched across the cut, he cautioned against ellipses: "In the change of images, no part of the movement should be lost." Kobitzsch discussed specific "postulates" for smoothing over the disorientation caused by a change of shots, such as cutting at an important phase of an action so that its continuation in the next shot would be clearly recognizable, or waiting for a pause in the action and then beginning with stillness in the next shot as well, which would "make the expression of the quiet moment the binding element." Perhaps most significantly, he treated "continuity of the direction of movement" (*Kontinuität der Bewegungsrichtung*) as another postulate: "It is one of the strongest means of binding images. The end of the image of an uncompleted movement is always abrupt, and the continuation after the interruption will be expected to be in the same direction (on the screen)." He also cautioned that the speed of the movement should be the same to prevent the cut from being perceived as creating a break in the action. Remarkably, Kobitzsch even includes overhead diagrams of where the camera should be placed for successive shots to keep continuous screen direction when a character moves through a doorway or goes around a corner.[21] Comparable diagrams had not yet appeared in American technical journals at this point, though one might assume that Hollywood editors knew the guidelines well enough not to need them.

Thus, apart from the stylistic changes that are so evident in the mainstream German films of the mid-1920s, we have ample testimony to the systematic influence of Hollywood films from the contemporary technical press. What sorts of influences were passed in the opposite direction – influences that may be more familiar from traditional historical accounts of the period?

Distinctively German Devices and Their Impact

When considering the German stylistic influence on Hollywood, most film scholars think immediately of the *enfesselte Kamera* ("unfastened camera"). While tripod-based camera movements such as pans and tracks had existed since nearly the beginning of the cinema, this new technique sought to free the camera, allowing it to move more fluidly, often leaving the ground and soaring through the air. The device probably originated in France, pioneered by the French Impressionists. Most notably, Jean Epstein placed a camera with a couple sitting in a whirling carnival-ride chair in Coeur fidèle (1923; Fig. 6.21).

Since Impressionist films were seldom widely exported, however, the Germans gained credit for the innovation - an view which has persisted to the present.

Although today the *entfesselte Kamera* is usually equated with a moving camera, a 1927 German article on the subject found other sorts of examples. It suggests that the exploitation of unusual angles or camera placements in an edited scene also exemplified the "unfastened camera" concept: "Even in America, which held fast to painterly image composition for a long time, the unfastened camera has created a school of thought. In BEN HUR, it was given its freedom. The race scene was a triumph of the camera. Cameras were placed on the floor of the arena, on automobiles, in airplanes, in the galleries – above all the camera reigned." The article is illustrated with a publicity photo for the 1927 MGM film THE SHOW, where an extreme high-angle shot is in itself taken to be an example of the *enfesselte Kamera*.[22] Indeed, the greater variety of extreme camera angles in Hollywood films after the mid-1920s may be as important an example of German influence as is camera movement.

The first notable German use of the *entfesselte Kamera* was in the 1923 film SYLVESTER (aka NEW YEAR'S EVE, directed by Lupu Pick). Here the camera executed relatively simple tracking movements, but independently of any figure. For example, at one point the camera glides through a large set of a city street (Figs. 6.22 and 6.23). Incidentally, this scene reflects the growing use of large spotlights for night scenes. SYLVESTER, a simple, gloomy *Kammerspiel* film of a sort that apparently only the Germans (and a few French intellectuals) could love, was not widely seen. Murnau's DER LETZTE MANN (1924), however, brought wide attention to the freely moving camera. Two of the most notable moments are the opening image of the large hotel lobby, with the camera descending inside an elevator and following figures out into the street, and the placement of the camera on a spinning turntable to suggest the protagonist's tipsiness. Perhaps the most famous shot was the rapid crane up from a trumpet's horn to a long shot of the musicians from a high window, conveying the protagonist's point of view and the notes of the trumpet flying up toward him (Figs. 6.24 and 6.25). Although THE LAST LAUGH was only moderately successful in the US, Hollywood filmmakers studied it closely. The revelations of the *entfesselte Kamera* were even more apparent in Dupont's VARIÉTÉ (1925), where the camera swung with circus performers on trapezes (Fig. 6.26). The *entfesselte Kamera* also filtered down into ordinary German films, often used in dancing scenes. The camera could follow revelers by either being handheld or placed on a moving platform of some sort. In a shot from HURRAH! ICH LEBE!, for example, the camera sits on a small merry-go-round in a nightclub, circling with it as the set and background characters move by (Fig. 6.27).

There was no specific camera support manufactured for this purpose, and intricate movements could require a fair amount of technical ingenuity and improvisation. Dupont described the elaborate means used for the trapeze shots in *Variété* in an article he wrote for the *New York Times* (in itself a good indication of broad American interest in the subject): "For one of the scenes we strapped a camera to another trapeze, facing Jannings, and operated it electrically from the ground. To make the following scene we lowered a camera by cable, slow-cranking all the way. We 'shot' from every angle in the theatre, using every device known and a great many that were invented at the moment."[23] In METROPOLIS, Lang famously rigged a simple hanging support to support the camera during a swinging camera movement rendering the impact of an explosion.

The *entfesslte Kamera's* impact can be seen occasionally in Hollywood films from 1926 on. The earliest devices for moving the camera through the air independently from a tripod or dolly were generally frameworks or platforms suspended from a track in the ceiling. "Tracking" shots above and along banquet tables appear in such films as FLESH AND THE DEVIL (1926), which has a number of "unfastened" movements. A swirling shot follows John Gilbert and Greta Garbo as they dance. During the duel scene a lengthy and fast pullback takes the camera into an extreme long shot with the duelists just outside the frame on either side. As the scene end, the smoke from their firing pistols bursts into the image (Figs. 6.28 and 6.29). Frank Borzage's crew used a tall elevator to move the camera with the protagonists as they went up seven flights of stairs in SEVENTH HEAVEN (1927). Use of the *enfesselte Kamera* for interiors reached its extreme point in 1929 with BROADWAY, for which Universal built a huge crane with an arm over 30 feet long and attached to a platform mounted on tires. It was used for a number of sweeping movements up and back to reveal the large, quasi-expressionistic nightclub set (Figs. 6.30 and 6.31). Perhaps the ultimate American example of the unfastened camera in this era, however, was WINGS (1927, William Wellman), with its spectacular aerial war footage shot by multiple cameras mounted on various parts of airplanes (Fig. 6.32).

In relation to this trend, Lubitsch was a typical Hollywood director, picking up influences from German films circulating in the US. Until 1926, he had been quite sparing with camera movements, but he began using them a bit more freely in 1927 with THE STUDENT PRINCE IN OLD HEIDELBERG. The opening scene contains a forward movement when a group of men in a tavern rise to salute a portrait of their king (Fig. 6.33); the camera moves over their heads (Fig. 6.34) up to a tight framing of the portrait. The camera was presumably suspended from an overhead track. His 1929 film, ETERNAL LOVE, which lies outside the purview of this book, contains many tracking shots and looks very Germanic in terms of design as well.

A second technique popularized by German films, the montage sequence, seems to have originated in that country, and Lubitsch helped to introduce it in the US. The superimpositions and rapid editing used by French Impressionist filmmakers may have been the inspiration for such montages, but the French had mainly used these devices to convey characters' subjective impressions. The influence of these kinds of subjective shots appears in Germany in as early as 1923, in DIE STRASSE, when the protagonist dreams of the exotic appeals of the mysterious streets outside his bourgeois apartment (Fig. 6.35). The loss or unavailability of many mid-1920s German films makes it hard to pin down exactly when the non-subjective montage sequence originated. Nevertheless, by 1926 German films were commonly using shots of various people and places grouped and superimposed within the same shot, not to express a characters state of mind but to summarize situations. This could be to suggest the passage of time, as in many of the more familiar montage sequences used in Hollywood in the 1930s. German filmmakers, however, typically used brief montages to sum up an ongoing situation by showing several characters in different spaces – perhaps a development of the split-screen telephone conversation so familiar in the international silent cinema from early in the century.

Typically the German montage sequence involves a group of images, often canted or otherwise presented from an unusual angle, scattered about the screen against a black background, and often overlapping and changing within what is essentially a single shot. A typical example can be seen in VOM TÄTER FEHLT JEDE SPUR (1928), where anonymous heads with telephones represent the issuing of a police alert (Fig. 6.36). A very similar shot is used in DER MANN IM FEUER (1926) for a fire alarm, with alarm buttons, a fireman with a phone, superimposed words, and the like (Fig. 6.37). Clearly this convenient way of telegraphing information quickly emerged as a convention. Evidence that this montage technique developed out of the telephone split-screen comes in a 1925 film, EINE ANSTÄNDIGE FRAU, where a police alert is shown by the more old-fashioned, conventional composition where a familiar image identifying a city (the Eiffel Tower) appears in the center, surrounded by small images of officials all receiving the same telegraph message, sent by a hand on a key at the bottom (Fig. 6.38). This particular split-screen shot is unusually elaborate, suggesting that filmmakers were ready to move on to a more abstract, compressed way of conveying the same thing – as in the shots from the two 1926 films mentioned above. Other German films of this period open with quick shots blending brightly lit signs to establish a city milieu, showing that montage sequences could be a modern-looking, efficient way of conveying story information.

Hollywood filmmakers were quick to recognize that for that very reason, montage sequences could be useful within the classical system. Such scenes soon began to appear in American films. Here Lubitsch was a pioneer. He employed a lively and elaborate montage sequence of moving camera, editing, and superimpositions to depict a large, drunken party in So This Is Paris. The sequence involves a kaleidoscopic lens of a type used fairly commonly in the 1920s and 1930s (Fig. 6.39), and it superimposes the face of a musician over the wild dancing (Fig. 6.40). That such passages were novel to American film-making is evidenced by two reviewers' detailed descriptions of the sequence and the audience's reaction to it during the film's August 13 premiere:

From the *New York Times*:
In "So This Is Paris," his tour de force is an extraordinarily brilliant conception of an eye full [sic] of a Charleston contest, with vibrant kaleidoscopic changes from feet and figures to the omnipotent saxophones. This dazzling episode is like the dream of a man drinking more than his share of wine at such an event. The comedy in this film had, up to that time, kept the audience in constant explosions of laughter, but the startling dissolving scenic effects and varied "shots" elicited a hearty round of applause.

From *Variety*:
For straightaway directorial novelty Lubitsch handles a Parisian ball scene in a manner only equaled by the freaky shot or two of "Variety." In the massive crowded ball room, splendid in its own way, Lubitsch runs in a mass of mazy and hazy feet and heads, figures and legs; ofttimes clear, at other times misty. Double exposures and a dozen other tricks are there with one shot prominent, a stretch of bare legs as though an entire chorus lined up with nothing but legs showing in front until the audience at the Cameo on the hottest night of the summer, involuntarily burst into applause.[24]

It should not be too surprising that Lubitsch would be so innovative, despite his easy assimilation into Hollywood-style filmmaking. Florey reported that during the production of Rosita, he had discussed "caligarisme," or Expressionism, with the director: "Ernst Lubitsch categorically declared to me that he was a partisan of all avant-garde ideas from the artistic point of view and that 'Caligari' had pleased him immensely."[25]

Because the montage sequence was so useful a narrational device, Hollywood adopted it. Another early case appears in Flesh and the Devil, which in general employs many German stylistic flourishes. The sequence compresses the protagonist's travels as he returns from exile to return to the woman he loves. The white letters of her name, "Felicitas," are superimposed initially over horses' running legs and then a train's rushing wheels – a scene not only indicating his progress but also suggesting that the eager man hears his lover's name in the rhythmic sounds of hooves and wheels (Fig. 6.41).

By 1927, montage sequences had become relatively common, especially in the opening moments of films. Not surprisingly, German and other émigré directors favored such scenes. Murnau's SUNRISE opens with an art title, "Summertime ... vacation time," that comes to life and leads into a montage of superimposed images of summer travel and activities; Figure 6.42 juxtaposes a low-angle shot of an ocean liner with a slight high-angle shot of a beach seen past a foreground bather. The film also contains subsequent montage sequences, as when the City Woman tempts the protagonist with a vision of urban pleasures. One scene in Leni's THE LAST WARNING (1928) shows a theater façade with newspaper reviews superimposed (Fig. 6.43). Paul Fejos's LONESOME (1928) conveys telephone calls with figures against a black background, much in the German fashion (Fig. 6.44). Thus it seems clear that, despite the term, "montage" sequences have little to do with influence from Soviet films. They appear in German and American films before filmmakers in those countries could have seen the first works of the Soviet Montage movement.

The third distinctively German trait that influenced Hollywood was set design. Historians have long claimed that Expressionism had an impact on 1930s horror films and 1940s films noirs. The latter claim is debatable, since, as we have seen, selective lighting with bright patches projected against darkness were common in Hollywood films before they came into widespread use in Germany. Clearly, however, some Universal horror films have a very Germanic look, most notably THE BLACK CAT (1934, Edgar G. Ulmer) and SON OF FRANKENSTEIN (1939, Rowland V. Lee). Perhaps more pervasive, however, was the adoption of German techniques of forced perspective and miniatures in sets. The street scenes in front of the Atlantic Hotel in DER LETZTE MANN use both techniques in a quite discernible way (Fig. 6.45). A sense of a vast street and buildings stretching away from the sidewalk are conveyed partly by distorted perspective in the long building stretching from the upper left into the "distance." Moreover, the people and cars bustling about in the background are actually small cutouts and/or models resting on moving belts. The lack of realism in these figures blends in with the slight stylization of the film's other sets. In FAUST, the vast landscape over which the protagonist and Mephistopheles fly on the magic carpet is patently a miniature, as are the cityscapes of METROPOLIS (Fig. 6.46). Murnau and designer Rochus Gliese applied similar techniques on a larger scale in the sets of SUNRISE. There was also a vogue in the late 1920s and early 1930s for beginning a film with a camera movement swooping over elaborate model buildings, as at the beginning of King Vidor's THE CROWD (1928). Perhaps the contrast of these unrealistic settings with the full-size objects and locales that occupied succeeding scenes led to a decline in this usage.

No doubt Germany developed some important and distinctive techniques during the 1920s, and no doubt these influenced Hollywood. The introduction of these techniques, however, took place during the period when German films were, on the whole, being Americanized. The spectacularly moving camera and the montage sequence both served the needs of classical storytelling, though they would never be more than occasional devices applied to a limited range of situations. Forced perspective and miniatures were fostered by the Expressionist movement, where houses and streets might be painted on flat surfaces, as in CALIGARI, or the ground might be tilted up toward the camera, as in DIE NIBELUNGEN. Hollywood practitioners had been using their own sort of forced perspective in the form of glass shots, paintings of buildings or landscapes on glass sheets through which the camera shot the full-scale settings; the elements on the glass (ideally) blended imperceptibly with the rest of the scene. (We saw a glass shot used to extend a set upward in ROSITA; see Fig. 3.36.) German techniques for exaggerating the apparent size of sets could obviously be added to Hollywood's bag of tricks for reducing construction costs. As has happened since nearly the earliest days of the cinema, American practitioners copied or adapted what was useful to them in the works of their overseas colleagues and ignored the rest. Hollywood cinema, however, had a more widespread and lasting influence on filmmaking in Germany during this period, and Ernst Lubitsch, perhaps more than any other, helped make it happen.

We have examined a set of favorable conditions for influence that allowed Lubitsch to adopt Hollywood filmmaking practice in Germany in 1921 and 1922. A sudden influx of films in a style strikingly different from the familiar German norm demonstrated that practice to him. His previous success within the German industry was strong enough to allow him to make films as he wished to. He also gained access to the technical means – the well-equipped EFA studio – that would allow him to replicate what he saw on the screen. Moreover, Lubitsch's stable situation, working for the same production company in the same facilities and with so many of the same cast and crew for so long, limits the number of likely explanations for the changes in the way he worked. Both acclaim in his own country and what we must suspect was his desire to win an invitation to work in Hollywood would reinforce his use of classical techniques.

Looking at the more general German filmmaking situation, we have been able to examine direct evidence of what technical means were available to Lubitsch and other directors and what norms governed craft choices during the postwar years. All of this evidence adds up to a particularly clear-cut case for the influence of Hollywood cinema on Lubitsch and on the German film industry as a whole.

Few situations in the history of the cinema offer such a straightforward case for influence as does post-World War I German filmmaking. Nevertheless, the sort of research presented here could also be undertaken for other countries, periods, industries, and filmmakers. In many situations, claims of American influence could be convincingly made.

Having made the case for Hollywood's influence on Lubitsch, however, there is one more subject that no one writing about this director can avoid mentioning and that is the "Lubitsch touch."

Epilogue: The Lubitsch Touch

Almost anyone writing about Lubitsch, from a journalistic or academic perspective, invokes "The Lubitsch Touch" as shorthand for some elusive quality that sets this director's work apart. The phrase is vague and usually not very helpful. Anyone who knows what it means already knows Lubitsch, and for someone who does not know Lubitsch, the phrase explains little. It is not likely, however, to go away, and for that reason it might be helpful to end by trying to pin it down just a little, both in terms of its meaning and its origins.

There is a popular impression that the Lubitsch Touch usually indicates a moment of sophisticated sexual innuendo, but in fact commentators tend to imply something more general. Even though Lubitsch is today far less known to the public than Hitchcock, Ford, or Hawks, filmmakers tend to retain an enormous amount of respect and affection for him. Peter Bogdanovich made this stab at defining the Touch:

> "The Lubitsch Touch" – it was as famous a moniker in its day as Hitchock's "Master of Suspense," though perhaps not as superficial. The phrase does connote something light, strangely indefinable, yet nonetheless tangible, and seeing Lubitsch's films – more than in almost any other director's work – one can feel this certain spirit; not only in the tactful and impeccably appropriate placement of the camera, the subtle economy of his plotting, the oblique dialog which had a way of saying everything through indirection, but also – and particularly – in the performance of every single player, no matter how small the role.[1]

Billy Wilder was a bit more specific:

> It was the elegant use of the Superjoke. You had a joke, and you felt satisfied, and then there was one more big joke on top of it. The joke you didn't expect. That was the Lubitsch touch ...
> Find some new way to tell your story. That was the magic of Lubitsch. He is eternally essential to me.[2]

Herman G. Weinberg's early study of Lubitsch, *The Lubitsch Touch*, helped to engrave the phrase in stone, and his definition of it is somewhat helpful:

> In its broadest sense, this meant going from the general to the particular, suddenly condensing into one swift, deft moment the crystallization of a scene or even the entire theme... the idea of utilizing the power of the metaphor by suddenly compressing the quintessence of his subject in a sly *comment* – a visual comment, naturally – that said it all.[3]

This notion of the touch consisting of individual, highly compressed moments comes fairly close to the use of the term during the 1920s, as we shall see. Weinberg also quotes Douglas Fairbanks, Jr., who says something fairly similar: "He accomplished his purpose in a style so recognizably his own that the phrase 'the Lubitsch touch,' used to describe a humorously oblique and sophisticated directorial device, became famous."[4]

It may be impossible to pin down the Lubitsch Touch, but we can at least look at how and when it originated and what it meant in those days. Its early formulation seems to have come in the mid-1920s, and in those days it was usually plural: Lubitsch touches.

The phrase is probably linked to the fact that by that period, Lubitsch was seen as having brought a new sophistication and subtlety to Hollywood filmmaking. A 1925 editorial in *The Film Daily* commented on the outstanding big-budget pictures of the year, but then continued:

> Yet there have been many splendid pictures, just in between the great ones, and far above the regular releases, and all of them have done much for the industry – [George] Fitzmaurice in "The Dark Angel" did it; Malcolm St. Clair is doing it for Famous [Players-Lasky], and Lubitsch, that wizard, is constantly doing it. What a school Lubitsch has established! His influence is noticed time and again in many pictures.[5]

The nature of that influence might be determined to some extent by looking at what contemporary critics meant by "Lubitsch touches."

I cannot claim to have made a thorough search for reviews of Lubitsch's films in the 1920s trade, fan, and local press. But a survey of the *New York Times*, *Variety*, *The Moving Picture World*, and *The Film Daily* reveals a clear time frame for the use of the term.

The earliest application of the word "touch" in these reviews that I found came in 1921, when the *New York Times*'s reviewer commented on DECEPTION (the American release title of ANNA BOLEYN). After remarking that Henny Porten was too old and heavy to play the young Anna, the reviewer continues: "There is nothing to suggest the quality of heaviness about Mr. Lubitsch, however. His work has a Continental touch."[6] There is nothing specific to Lubitsch in this usage. Still, given that "the Lubitsch touch" often stands in for a type of sophistication not thought typical of American cinema, the phrase may derive from the cliché of "the Continental touch."

This early review, however, did not apparently herald the immediate linkage of "touch" and "Lubitsch." It seems to be in 1924, in reference to THREE WOMEN and FORBIDDEN PARADISE, that such touches are mentioned regularly in reviews, and they only occasionally imply a "Continental" taste for risqué innuendo. Here, for example, a review of Kiss Me Again lauds Lubitsch simply for subtlety:

> "Kiss Me Again" has many deft and delightful touches, the outstanding one being where Mr. Lubitsch depicts a rain shower in a natural way. The average director resorts to a deluge after a glimpse of darkening skies torn by streaks of lightning. Mr. Lubitsch craftily shows a few spots of rain on the pavement, and even when the shower comes, it is pictured as an ordinary rainfall and not as a cloud burst.[7]

Unfortunately Kiss Me Again is lost, and we cannot assess this claim, nor the one by another reviewer concerning a decidedly risqué moment in this same film: "There is a touch that will cause audiences to gasp when they get the suggestion of the two disrobing. It is cleverly done, and at the finish there is a touch that takes away all the suggestiveness."[8]

Lubitsch touches were often associated with comedy of a sophisticated sort. *The Film Daily*'s reviewer noted generally of So This Is Paris that it is "A sophisticated and amusing entanglement of life in Paris, replete with those charming touches which Lubitsch knows how to do so well ... So This Is Paris very closely shows the Lubitsch hand. His touches tickle the risibilities. They induce chuckles first, then giggles and then outright laughter."[9] Yet the touches were not invariably comic. A comment on Three Women suggests that "touches" can imply subtlety or comedy (or presumably both at once): "Mr. Lubitsch's direction is marked by the same subtle touches, the same unerring ability to portray human nature, its fine points and its frailties; the same touches of comedy ..."[10] In 1926, the *New York Times*'s reviewer summarized Lubitsch's talent for adding memorable "strokes" to his films by pointing to three cases from three different films:

> No matter how brilliant may be the picture Mr. Lubitsch produces, he succeeds invariably in inserting a transcendental stroke. Few will forget that brilliant scene in which a fish rippled through the reflection of the lovers about to embrace in "Forbidden Paradise." In "Kiss Me Again" Mr. Lubitsch portrayed a rain shower without calling for a flood of water, and in the film translation of "Lady Windermere's Fan" he denoted haste in writing a note by having a wet blot of ink on the paper.[11]

One review of Lady Windermere's Fan uses the term both in the singular and the plural, and here the implication seems to be that Lubitsch touches might add a bit too much sophistication to his films: "Lubitsch with his masterful touch has turned this somewhat weak material for pictures into a very fine production replete with typical Lubitsch touches, but whether or not it is over the heads of the average picture audience remains to be seen."[12] Indeed, a common complaint from small-town exhibitors was that Lubitsch films, while excellent, often did not appeal to their patrons due to this sophistication.

Lubitsch touches as perceived by reviewers seem often to have involved bits of business given to the actors, sometimes in combination with the editing. In a lukewarm review of LADY WINDERMERE'S FAN, the *Variety* reviewer nevertheless remarked on the "clever touches of the director's art furnished by Lubitsch"; the moments he singled out were these:

> Lubitsch in handling the scenes at the race track did most effective work, and the shots taken from the window in the apartment in which the wife sees her husband dismiss his own car and hail a taxi were also clever, as were the subsequent scenes with Miss McAvoy. Lubitsch had her use her hands in a manner that focused [the] attention of the audience on them and they reflected most cleverly the emotions that the youthful actress was passing through. This was by far his best piece of direction in the picture.[13]

Another reviewer found a completely different set of scenes from the same film to single out:

> Mr. Lubitsch has contributed several clever and distinctly individual touches, such as a progressive blocking off of the screen as the bachelor overtakes Mrs. Erlynne, the sudden bobbing up of the heads of the three dowagers when she appears at the ball, the unexpected and amusing handling of Lord Darlington's declaration of love for Lady Windermere and the deft way he assists the Lord to retrieve an incriminating letter, also the rather risqué touches showing the development of the affair between the bachelor and Mrs. Erlynne.[14]

The "progressive blocking off of the screen" referred to here is a famous tracking shot at the end of the racetrack scene, which utilizes a moving mask. As the preceding shot begins, Mrs. Erlynne appears at the right, leaving the racetrack (Fig. E.1). After she exits left, the bachelor enters from the right, following her (Fig. E.2). The next shot again begins with Mrs. Erlynne, but now the camera tracks with her. Soon the bachelor appears, walking faster than she (Fig. E.3), and as he catches up to her, a dark mask slides across the frame behind him (Fig. E.4).

One reviewer discussing THE STUDENT PRINCE IN OLD HEIDELBERG, though not using the term "touch," points to a scene which he takes to be typical of Lubitsch's directorial style back as far as the German period:

> The first suggestions of the director who made "Passion," "The Marriage Circle" and other pictures comes when a throng of frock-coated and silk-hatted men simultaneously uncover their heads in honor of the princeling. Mr. Lubitsch, who is always ready with his contrasting bits, skips to an elderly man dozing in a chair, who just doffs his hat but without permitting it to interfere with the enjoyment of his siesta.[15]

All these uses of the term suggest that Lubitsch's habitual attempt to tell a story visually and to minimize the use of intertitles created a style that utilized the norms of classical filmmaking but was also recognizable to contemporaries as distinctively his own. The touches created moments that were more subtle, more sophisticated, more memorable, more unexpected, more original, and sometimes more risqué.

Perhaps one of the best descriptions of what would come to be generally known as the Lubitsch touch was, oddly enough, written in 1924, before the term itself had become widespread – possibly before it had even been used. This description came from an exhibitor in Oklahoma City. In a regular *Moving Picture World* column designed for exhibitors to report to each other concerning the success or failure they experienced with specific films, William Noble, of the Criterion Theatre, seemed to forget the terse format of most reports and waxed eloquent over THE MARRIAGE CIRCLE:

> A delicious dilemma with the double deviltry of the wrong wife after the wrong husband. Lubitsch is noted as a great motion picture producer. He is uncannily deft, stripping the drama till its very life essence is unfolded and the unnecessary eliminated. His master hand deftly weaves the delicate skein of the involved relationship of the characters into an intricate web. With relentless analysis, with subtle humor and with a general outlook on life as different from the accepted standard as it is intrigueing [sic] he gives an intimate and true conception and representation of contemporary life. The result, in "The Marriage Circle," is a photoplay of magic-holding powers, with the property of entertaining the audience from the very beginning to the last fade out.[16]

My goal here has not been to pin down when the director's approach would be encapsulated in the singular as "the Lubitsch touch." That seems to have happened well into the sound era. In a brief essay published in 1933, Lubitsch wrote, "I am constantly asked: 'How do you decide on those touches that stamp a film?'" and in the same essay Lubitsch also seems to imply that each individual film has "a different touch." [17] Thus Lubitsch himself apparently saw the term as describing, not his overall style, but a set of tactics characteristic of his work. Perhaps the best way to define the Lubitsch touch is to say that it consists of all the many Lubitsch touches he invented during his splendid career.

Notes

Notes to Introduction

1. "Ernst Lubitsch: A Symposium," *The Screen Writer* 3, 8 (January, 1948): 16.
2. Peter Bogdanovich, "Introduction," *Who the Devil Made It?* (New York: Alfred A. Knopf, 1997), pp. 30-37. The passage quoted is on page 30.
3. Cameron Crowe, *Conversations with Wilder* (New York: Alfred A. Knopf, 1999), p. 192.
4. Cameron Crowe, "Leave 'em Laughing," *Newsweek* Special issue on comedy (Summer, 1998): 23-24.
5. Kristin Thompson, *Exporting Entertainment: America in the World Film Market, 1907-1934* (London: The British Film Institute, 1985).
6. Paul Rotha, *The Film Till Now* 3rd ed. (Feltham, Middlesex: Spring Books, 1967), pp. 252-253.
7. Arthur Knight, *The Liveliest Art* (New York: Macmillan, 1957), p. 62.

Notes to Chapter One

1. Jurij Tynjanov, "On Literary Evolution," tr. C. A. Luplow, in Ladislav Matejka and Krystyna Pomorska, eds., *Readings in Russian Poetics: Formalist and Structuralist Views* (Cambridge, Mass.: MIT Press, 1971), p. 76.
2. For the best account of Lubitsch's early career, see Hans Helmut Prinzler, "Berlin, 29.1.1892 – Hollywood, 30.11.1947," in Hans Helmut Prinzler and Enno Patalas, eds., *Lubitsch* (Munich: C. J. Bucher, 1984), Part One, pp. 8-35. Prinzler lists all the plays in which Lubitsch acted on pp. 3-14 and 18-19. I quote from the latter, p. 19.
3. Jan-Christopher Horak, *Ernst Lubitsch and the Rise of UFA 1917-1922* (Unpublished MS thesis, Boston: Boston University, 1975), pp. 7-19. Horak's thesis remains the primary study of Lubitsch's relationship to the German film industry. I am grateful to him for having supplied me with a copy of it.
4. Horak, pp. 32-63.
5. Horak, pp. 21-22, 64-70.
6. Horak, p. 95.
7. Scott Eyman treats both films dismissively and suggests that *Romeo und Julia im Schnee* "has the feel of a throwaway, something Lubitsch was not fully engaged by." See his *Ernst Lubitsch: Laughter in Paradise* (New York: Simon & Schuster, 1993), pp. 67-68.
8. The calculations were made by Kurt Pinthus in *Das Tage-Buch*. See Klaus Kreimeier, *The Ufa Story: A History of German's Greatest Film Company 1918-1945* tr. Robert and Rita Kimber (New York: Hill and Wang, 1996), p. 59.

9. For brief descriptions of the Union-Glashaus and its environs, see Hans-Michael Bock, "Berliner Ateliers: Ein kleines Lexikon," in Uta Berg-Ganschow and Wolfgang Jacobsen, eds., ... Film ... Stadt ... Kino ... Berlin (Berlin: Argon, 1987), pp. 197-199; and Hans-Michael Bock, "Die Glashäuser: Ateliergelände Tempelhof," in Hans-Michael Bock and Michael Tötenberg, eds., Das Ufa-Buch (Frankfurt am Main: Zweitausendeins, 1992), pp. 22-23.

10. Horak, pp. 105-107.

11. Lubitsch quoted in Der Film in early 1921, just after the founding of his production company. Quoted in Horak, p. 107.

12. Horak, pp. 107-108; Reimar Kuntze, "Die deutschen Filmateliers und ihre technische Ausrüstung," Die Filmtechnik 2, 12 (June 12, 1926): 240; Hans-Michael Bock, "Berliner Ateliers: Ein kleines Lexikon," in ... Film ... Stadt ... Kino ... Berlin ... (Berlin: Argon, 1987), p. 202.

13. Herbert Howe, "The Film Wizard of Europe," Photoplay (December 1922): 96.

14. "Lubitsch Due Here to Study American Methods," Moving Picture World 53, 9 (December 31, 1921): 1075.

15. Sumner Smith, "Ernst Lubitsch Describes Novel Method of Preparing a Picture for Production," Moving Picture World 54, 1 (January 7, 1922): 53.

16. Robert Florey, Deux ans dans les studios américains (Paris: Publications Jean-Pascal, 1926), p. 119. Despite the publication date, this book was a collection of magazine articles published earlier.

17. Robert Florey, La lanterne magique (Lausanne: La Cinémathèque Suisse, 1966), pp. 84; Eyman, Ernst Lubitsch, p. 87; Ali Hubert, Hollywood: Legende und Wirklichkeit (Leipzig: E. A. Seemann, 1930), pp. 46-47.

18. The myth of their feud stems mainly from her interview with Kevin Brownlow for The Parade's Gone By. There Pickford "quotes" whole conversations from decades earlier, painting a picture of disagreement on the set from the start. Her distaste for Rosita led her to try to suppress it, with the result that the only surviving version known today originated from a print preserved in the Soviet national archive. See Kevin Brownlow, The Parade's Gone By (New York: Knopf, 1968), pp. 129-134.

19. Eyman, pp. 92-95.

20. United Artists Collection, Wisconsin Center for Film and Theater Research, State Historical Society of Wisconsin, Madison. All of these pieces of correspondence are in the O'Brien Legal File, 99AN/2A, Box 209, Folder 13.

21. "Lubitsch to Direct," Moving Picture World (September 1, 1923): 68.

22. From a letter quoted in Eyman, Ernst Lubitsch, p. 121.

23. "Director Lubitsch Also Has an Eye for Business," Moving Picture World 64, 3 (September 15, 1923): 276.

24. Prinzler, "Berlin," p. 38; Eyman Ernst Lubitsch, 97.

25. Richard Koszarski, An Evening's Entertainment: The Age of the Silent Feature Picture, 1915-1928 (New York: Charles Scribner's Sons, 1990), p. 90.

26. "40 from Warners," Film Daily 33, 74 (September 25, 1925): 1-2.

27. Cables quoted in Rudy Behlmer, Inside Warner Bros. (1935-1951) (New York: Viking, 1985), pp. 335-337. See also Eyman, 115-124.

28. Sime. "So This Is Paris," Variety Film Reviews (New York: Garland, 1983), n.p. (August 18, 1926).

29. "Lubitsch Signs with Famous Players-Lasky," *Moving Picture World* 81, 6 (August 14, 1926): 7.
30. "Warners Sell Balance of Lubitsch Contract," *Moving Picture World* 82, 1 (September 4, 1926): 3.
31. Eithne and Jean-Loup Bourget, *Lubitsch ou la satire romanesque* (Paris: Stock, 1987), p. 23. Siegfried Kracauer used this "European Griffith" tag, citing Lewis Jacobs' *The Rise of the American Film*. See *From Caligari to Hitler* (Princeton: Princeton University Press, 1947), p. 51, fn. 23. Thus are historical clichés perpetuated.
32. Howe, "The Film Wizard of Europe," p. 28.
33. Leed. "Passion," *Variety Film Reviews* (New York: Garland, 1983), I, n.p. (December 17, 1920).
34. Eyman, *Ernst Lubitsch*, p. 160.
35. "Lubitsch Signs with Famous Players-Lasky," *Moving Picture World* 81, 7 (August 14, 1926): 2.
36. "Star and Director Guests of the Warners in New York," *Moving Picture World* 76, 7 (October 24, 1925): 634.
37. "Unique Honor for Lubitsch," *Moving Picture World* 79, 1 (March 6, 1926): 2.
38. "The Student Prince," *Moving Picture World* 88, 4 (September 24, 1927): 250.
39. Martin Dickstein, "Slow Motion," *Brooklyn Eagle* (September 25, 1927). Jean Hersholt collection, Margaret Herrick Library, scrapbook #8, p. 49.
40. John Loder, "A Monarch of the Cinema," *Film Weekly* (November 4, 1932), rep. in Thomas Elsaesser, ed., *Space Frame Narrative: Silent Cinema 1916-26: Ernst Lubitsch* (Norwich: University of East Anglia Film Studies, 1983), p. 156.
41. Memo from Mr. Krohner to Carl Laemmle, November 8, 1926, reproduced in Koszarski, *An Evening's Entertainment*, pp. 212-213. This memo did not include D. W. Griffith and Cecil B. De Mille, who had their own production companies.

Notes to Chapter Two

1. Ernst Lubitsch, "American Cinematographers Superior Artists," *American Cinematographer* 4, 9 (December, 1923): 18. By the way, I am fairly sure that Lubitsch wrote this himself; it deals with concerns similar to those that appear in articles he had published in Germany.
2. This comparison is based primarily on German and American cinematography manuals and technical trade journals for this period. The main journals for the US are *American Cinematographer* (1921 on) and *The Transactions of the Society of Motion Picture Engineers* (1916 on; *The Journal of the Society of Motion Picture Engineers* from 1930 on.) Those for Germany are *Die Kinotechnik* (1919 on) and *Die Filmtechnik* (1925 on).
3. Guido Seeber, *Der praktische Kameramann* (1927; rept. Frankfurt am Main: Deutsche Filmmuseum, 1980). Unless otherwise noted, all illustrations of German lighting equipment come from the section entitled "Die künstliche Beleuchtung für Filmaufnahmen," pp. 251-274.

4.   Carl Gregory, *Motion Picture Photography* (New York: Falk Publishing, 1927), oppo-
     site p. 220. Unless otherwise noted, all illustrations of American lighting equip-
     ment are from this book.
5.   Lubitsch, "American Cinematographers," p. 18.
6.   Seeber, *Der praktische Kameramann*, p. 268.
7.   Diagram from Hans Schmidt, *Kino-Taschenbuch für Amateure und Fachleute* (Berlin:
     Union deutsche Verlagsgesellschaft, 1921), p. 44. Interestingly, Schmidt repro-
     duces this diagram without change in the second edition of this book (same press,
     1926), p. 87.
8.   William Roy Mott, "White Light for Motion Picture Photography," *Transactions of
     the Society of Motion Picture Engineers* no. 8 (April 14-16, 1919), p. 32.
9.   Robert Florey, *Deux ans dans les studios américains* (Pris: Publications Jean-Pascal,
     1926), p. 19.
10. Carl Gregory, ed., *Condensed Course in Motion Picture Photography* (New York: New
     York Institute of Photography, 1920), opposite p. 228.
11. Wiard B. Ihnen and D. W. Atwater, "Artistic Utilization of Light in Motion Picture
     Photography," *Transactions of the Society of Motion Picture Engineers* no. 21 (May 18-
     21, 1925), p. 24.
12. Ihnen and Atwater, "Artistic Utilization of Light," p. 32.
13. Ihnen and Atwater, "Artistic Utilization of Light," p. 31.
14. Reproduced from Hans-Michael Bock and Michael Töteberg, *Das Ufa-Buch* Frank-
     furt am Main: Zweitausendeins, 1992), p. 23.
15. "Die erste Mary Pickford-Film," *Lichtbildbühne* 14, 9 (February 26, 1921): 20.
16. Florey, *Deux ans dans les studios américains*, p. 121.
17. Uta Berg-Ganschow and Wolfgang Jacobsen, ... *Film ... Stadt ... Kino ... Berlin ...*
     (Berlin: Argon, 1987), p. 202. F. W. Murnau had filmed *Der Januskopf* and *Die Gang
     in der Nacht* in this studio in 1920.
18. "Was die 'L.B.B.' erzählt," *Lichtbildbühne* 14, 18 (April 30, 1921): 61.
19. Karl J. Fritsch, "Meine Eindrücke in Amerika," *Lichtbildbühne* 15, 19 (May 6, 1922):
     29.
20. Karl J. Fritsch, "Die Aussichten für den deutschen Filmexport," *Lichtbildbühne*
     Luxusnummer (June 17, 1922): n.p.

Notes to Chapter Three

1.   Kenneth MacGowan, "Enter-the Artist," *Photoplay* 14, 1 (January 1921): 74.
2.   Jerome Lachenbruch, "Interior Decoration for the 'Movies': Studies from the Work
     of Cedric Gibbons and Gilbert White," *Arts and Decoration* 14, 3 (January, 1921):
     204.
3.   Hugo Balin, "The Scenic Background," *The Mentor* 9, 6 (July 1, 1921): 22.
4.   MacGowan, "Enter-the Artist," p. 74.
5.   Julius Urgiss, "Künstlerprofil: Ernst Lubitsch," *Der Kinematograph* (August 30,
     1916; rep. in Hans Helmut Prinzler and Enno Patalas, eds., *Lubitsch* (Munich:
     Bucher, 1984), p. 89.

6. See, for example, Jan-Christopher Horak's comments in *Ernst Lubitsch and the Rise of UFA 1917-1922*. Unpublished MS thesis (Boston: Boston University, 1975), p. 84.

7. Ernst Lubitsch, Letter to Herman G. Weinberg (20th Century-Fox), July 10, 1947, *Film Culture* no. 25 (Summer 1962), p. 39. This piece is often cited with a title, but there is none in the original publication, since the letter on studio letterhead is simply reproduced.

8. Eithne and Jean-Loup Bourget, *Lubitsch ou la satire Romanesque* (Paris: Stock, 1987), pp. 45-48.

9. James Cruze's *Beggar on Horseback*, made for Paramount in 1924, used somewhat comparable stylized comic sets. The film was widely considered arty and obscure; it was a box-office failure. On the occasional use of stylized sets in Hollywood films of the silent era, see my "The Limits of Experimentation in Hollywood," in Jan-Christopher Horak, ed., *Lovers of Cinema: The First American Avant-Garde* (Madison: University of Wisconsin Press, 1995), pp. 67-93.

10. Horak, *Lubitsch*, p. 72. On the high budget and sets, see also Pola Negri, *Memoirs of a Star* (Garden City, NY: Doubleday, 1970), pp. 140-141.

11. C.A.L., "Technische Bemerkungen zu 'Madame Dubarry,'" *Die Kinotechnik* 3, 8 (July 1921): 294.

12. The practice of introducing a deep set by drawing aside a foreground curtain had been common during the mid- to late-1910s. By this point it might be considered somewhat conventional. See my "The International Exploration of Cinematic Expressivity," in Karel Dibbets and Bert Hogenkamp, eds., *Film and the First World War* (Amsterdam: Amsterdam University Press, 1995), pp. 77-79.

13. Lubitsch saw *Orphans of the Storm* during its first run when he was in New York in 1922. He was reportedly "enthusiastic about it." See Herbert Howe, "The Film Wizard of Europe," *Photoplay* (December, 1922): 96.

14. Ernst Stern, *My Life, My Stage* (London: Victor Gollancz, 1951), pp. 182-183. Stern presumably studied hieroglyphs using the great German Egyptologist Jean Pierre Adolphe Erman's pioneering *Die Hieroglyphen* (1912, rep. 1917).

15. Stern, *My Life, My Work*, p. 182. On the budget of *Das Weib des Pharao*, see Jan-Christopher Horak, *Ernst Lubitsch and the Rise of UFA 1917-1922* (Unpublished MS thesis, Boston: Boston University, 1975), p. 111. On the whole Lubitsch's German films had used relatively few miniature settings, but at least two are apparent in *Sumurun*.

16. Rather confusingly, the artistic design of *Rosita* is credited to William Cameron Menzies, while Svend Gade is listed as set designer. What exactly this distinction meant in 1923 is unclear. The large prison set, however, definitely resembles the exotic sets designed by Mendies for *The Thief of Bagdad*. Perhaps we can assume that the set-designing duties were split between the two credited artists.

17. Robert Florey, *Deux ans dans les studios américains* (Paris: Publications Jean-Pascal, 1926), p. 158.

18. Robert Florey, *La lanterne magique* (Lausanne: La Cinémathèque Suisse, 1966), p. 90.

19. "'The Marriage Circle,'" *The Film Daily* (February 10, 1924): 5.

20. "'Susceptible Men,'" *New York Times* (February 4 1924); rep. in *The New York Times Film Reviews 1913-1968* (New York: New York Times and Arno Press, 1970), vol. 1, p. 184.

21. For example: "The constant rhythmical use of doors as narrative instruments is one of the distinctive indicators of Lubitsch's style." See Mario Verdone, *Ernst Lubitsch* (Paris: Premier Plan, 1964), p. 40 = *Premier Plan* 32.

22. Harold Grieve, "Background Stuff," *The Motion Picture Director* 3, 3 (November-December, 1926): 29.

23. Grieve, "Background Stuff," pp. 28-29. *The Skyrocket* was directed by Marshall Neilan and released five months before *So This Is Paris*.

24. Mordaunt Hall, "An Oscar Wilde Play," *The New York Times Film Reviews* (December 28, 1925), Vol. 1, p. 290.

25. Mordaunt Hall, "Mr. Lubitsch's Direction Outshines His Narrative," *The New York Times* (October 12, 1924), rep. in George Pratt, ed., *Spellbound in Darkness: A History of the Silent Film* (rev. ed; Greenwich, Conn.: New York Graphic Society, 1973), p. 319.

26. Adolf Höllriegel, *Hollywood Bilderbuch* (1927), quoted in Prinzler and Patalas, *Lubitsch* pp. 41-42.

27. Howe, "The Film Wizard of Europe," p. 98.

28. Ernst Lubitsch, as told to William Stull, ASC, "Concerning Cinematography: A Few Words from Ernst Lubitsch on Cinematic Conditions," *American Cinematographer* (November 1929); rep. *American Cinematographer* 75, 8 (August, 1994): 71.

Notes to Chapter Four

1.   David Bordwell, Janet Staiger, and Kristin Thompson, *The Classical Hollywood Cinema: Film Style and Mode of Production to 1960* (New York: Columbia University Press, 1985), p. 285.

2.   I have written about the division of labor in German and other European studios in the late silent era in "Early Alternatives to the Hollywood Mode of Production: Implications for Europe's Avant-gardes," *Film History* 5, 4 (1993): 386-404.

3.   Herbert Howe, "The Film Wizard of Europe," *Photoplay* (December 1922): 98.

4.   Quoted in Scott Eyman, *Ernst Lubitsch: Laughter in Paradise* (New York: Simon & Schuster, 1993), p. 207.

5.   Kristin Thompson, "The International Exploration of Cinematic Expressivity," in Karel Dibbets and Bert Hogencamp, eds., *Film and the First World War* (Amsterdam: Amsterdam University Press, 1995), pp. 81-83; Kristin Thompson, "Stylistic Expressivity in *Die Landstrasse*," in Thomas Elsaesser, ed., *A Second Life: German Cinema's First Decades* (Amsterdam: Amsterdam University Press, 1996), pp. 260-262.

6.   At last two historians have attributed a knowledge of these continuity editing principles to German filmmakers of the early 1920s. Noël Burch states that Fritz Lang was among the German filmmakers most expert at applying those principles:

     Gradually, between 1907 and 1917, it became possible to maintain the illusion of continuity while resorting to fragmentation (to *decoupage*), and to impose the illusion so strongly that the very existence of shot changes, like the edges of the frame, became to-tally obscured.

By 1922, every practicing film-maker was more or less familiar with this system of ori-entation, though few of them so thoroughly as Fritz Lang.

Burch goes on to analyze how *Dr. Mabuse der Spieler* exhibits extremely adept edit-ing of the classical sort. See his *In and Out of Synch: The Awakening of a Cine-dreamer* (Aldershot: Scolar Press, 1991), pp. 6-7.

In his history of editing, Don Fairservice points out that many German filmmakers immediately after the war displayed no knowledge of the 180-degree system. A short time later, however, he argues that some filmmakers were so cognizant of it that they were able to exploit occasional across-the-line cuts for dramatic effect. He singles out Murnau's *Nosferatu* (1922), saying that it primarily observes the 180-degree rule but also occasionally deliberately breaks it. See Fairservice's *Film Editing: History, Theory and Practice* (Manchester: Manchester University Press, 2001), pp. 89-91.

Although Fairservice does not mention it, *Nosferatu* also makes impressive use of false eyeline matches. For example, at one point Ellen seems to "see" the vampire, many miles away, about to attack her husband, Hutter; she holds out her arms in appeal, and in the next shot, the vampire turns away from Hutter and looks off right, as if responding to her. Such imaginative use of a continuity devise suggests a considerable grasp of Hollywood-style editing.

Neither historian indicates how German filmmakers achieved their knowledge of continuity principles, and each concentrates on one of the most famous films of the era – both, coincidentally, from 1922. Burch seems to assume that a knowledge of continuity principles developed at the same rate internationally and makes no attempt to trace the conditions of influence. Similarly, Fairservice does not indi-cate what might have happened between the late 1910s and 1922 that would have permitted the deliberate violation of continuity rules. Neither mentions Lubitsch.

7. For a brief analysis of the racetrack scene and other passages of editing in *Lady Windermere's Fan*, see David Bordwell, *Narration in the Fiction Film* (Madison: Uni-versity of Wisconsin Press, 1985), pp. 178-186.

8. Charles S. Sewell, "Three Women," *Moving Picture World* 70, 4 (27 September 1924): 334.

9. Ernst Lubitsch, "Film Directing," in Clarence Winchester, ed., *The World Film Ency-clopedia* (London: The Amalgamated Press, 1933), p. 443.

Notes to Chapter Five

1. David Bordwell, Janet Staiger, and Kristin Thompson *The Classical Hollywood Cin-ema: Film Style and Mode of Production to 1960* (London: Routledge & Kegan Paul, 1985), pp. 189-192.

2. See Ben Brewster and Lea Jacobs, *Theatre to Cinema* (Oxford: Oxford University Press, 1997), Chapter 6 and 9; David Bordwell, *On the History of Film Style* (Cam-

bridge, MA: Harvard University Press, 1997), pp. 178-198; Bordwell, "La Nouvelle Mission de Feuillade, or, What Was Mise-en-Scéne?" *The Velvet Light Trap* 37 (1996): 10-29; and further consideration of Feuillade in his *Figures Traced in Light: On Cinematic Staging* (Berkeley: University of California Press, 2005), Chapter 2.

3. For a brief analysis of Hofer's staging, see Yuri Tsivian, "Two 'Stylists' of the Teens: Franz Hofer and Yevgenii Bauer," in *A Second Life: German Cinema's First Decades*, ed. Thomas Elsaesser (Amsterdam: Amsterdam University Press, 1996), pp. 270-274.

4. On Italian divas, see Ben Brewster and Lea Jacobs, *Theatre to Cinema* (Oxford: Oxford University Press, 1997), pp. 111-116; on the slow pace of Russian acting, see Yuri Tsivian, "Some Preparatory Remarks on Russian Cinema," in Paolo Cherchi Usai, Lorenzo Codelli, Carlo Montanaro, and David Robinson, eds., *Silent Witnesses: Russian Films 1908-1919* (London: British Film Institute, 1989), pp. 26-34, and also Brewster and Jacobs, pp. 124-126.

5. Hans Helmut Prinzler and Enno Patalas, eds., *Lubitsch* (Munich: Bucher, 1984), p. 25.

6. Jan-Christopher Horak, *Ernst Lubitsch and the Rise of UFA 1917-1922* Unpublished MA thesis, 1975 (Boston: Boston University), p. 84.

7. Asta Nielsen, *Die schweigende Muse*, uncredited translation from Danish (1946; Munich: Carl Hanser, 1977), pp. 293, 295.

8. Eithne and Jean-Loup Bourget, *Lubitsch ou la satire Romanesque* (Paris: Stock, 1987), p. 13.

9. "Passion," *New York Times* (December 13, 1920), rep. In George Pratt, ed., *Spellbound in Darkness*, rev. ed. (Greenwich, CT,: New York Graphic Society, 1973), p. 308.

10. Scott Eyman, *Ernst Lubitsch: Laughter in Paradise* (New York: Simon & Schuster, 1993), pp. 56, 67.

11. See Prinzler and Patalas, *Lubitsch*, where the authors list Lubitsch's roles as part of the Reinhardt Ensemble on pages 13-14 and 18-19. In their opinion, "he never played a really important role there," p. 19.

12. Horak, *Ernst Lubitsch*, p. 98.

13. "The Screen," *New York Times* (October 21, 1921), rep. In *New York Times Film Reviews 1913-1968* (New York: New York Times & Arno Press, 1970), Vol. 1: 104.

14. *"One Arabian Night,"* *Variety* (October 7, 1921): 43.

15. Herbert Howe, "The Film Wizard of Europe," *Photoplay* (December, 1922): 29.

16. Ernst Lubitsch, "Uns fehlen Filmdichtungen," in *Werkstadt Film: Selbstverständnis und Visionene von Filmleuten der zwanziger Jahre*, Rolf Aurich and Wolfgang Jacobsen, eds. (Munich: edition text + kritic, 1998), p. 57. Reprinted from *Das Tage-Buch* no. 35 (September 11, 1920).

17. On Mayer, see Horst Claus, "Backstairs Shattered: Comment on the Context of Two Kammerspiel Productions, *Scherben* and *Hintertreppe*" and Hermann Kappelhoff, "Literary Exploration of the Cinematographic Image," in Michael Omasta, Brigitte Mayr, and Christian Cargnelli, *Carl Mayer Scenar[t]ist* (Vienna: Synema, 2003), pp. 129-154 and 169-184.

18. Fred, "Rosita," *Variety* (September 6, 1923): 22.

19. Robert Florey, *Deux ans dans les studios américains* (Paris: Publications Jean-Pascal, 1926), pp. 161-162.

20. Robert Florey, *La lanterne magique* (Lausanne: La Cinémathèque Suisse, 1966), p. 89.

21. Quoted in Eyman, *Ernst Lubitsch*, p. 119.

22. Ali Hubert, *Hollywood: Legende und Wirklichkeit* (Leipzig: E.A. Seemann, 1930), p. 35.

23. Peter Bogdanovich, *Who the Devil Made It?* (New York: Alfred A. Knopf, 1997), pp. 32-33.

24. Eyman, *Ernst Lubitsch*, pp. 114, 102.

25. United Artists Collection, O'Brien Legal Files 99AN/2A, Box 209, Folder 14. Folders 13 and 14 contain numerous financial statements of payments to Pickford generated by her older films, still in release; these went back to *Suds* (1920). The point about *The Thief of Bagdad* and *America* was that if they were initially road shown, they would not be turned over to United Artists for regular release for quite some time. Chaplin did not release another film until *The Gold Rush* in 1925. Pickford, seemingly the financial mainstay of the company at this point, had *Dorothy Vernon of Haddon Hall* ready for a March 15, 1924 premiere.

26. Jim Tully, "Ernst Lubitsch," *Vanity Fair* (December 1926): 82.

27. Adolphe Menjou, with M. M. Musselman, *It Took Nine Tailors* (New York: Whittlesey House, 1948), pp. 110-111, 135-136.

28. Fred, "*The Marriage Circle*," *Variety* (February 7, 1924): 22.

29. Charles S. Sewell, "*The Marriage Circle*," *Moving Picture World* 66, 7 (February 16, 1924): 580.

30. C. S. Sewell, "'Forbidden Paradise,'" *Moving Picture World* 71, 5 (November 29, 1924): 448.

31. "Susceptible Men," *New York Times* (February 4, 1924), rep. In *The New York Times Film Reviews*, vol. 1, p. 184.

32. Sewell, "*The Marriage Circle*," p. 580.

33. Iris Barry, *Let's Go to the Pictures* (London: Chatto & Windus, 1926), p. 204.

34. C. S. Sewell, "*Lady Windermere's Fan*: Warner Brothers," *Moving Picture World* 77, 6 (December 12, 1925): 575.

35. "*Lady Windermere's Fan*," *Film Daily* (December 6, 1925): 4.

36. Mordaunt Hall, "Lubitsch Rings the Bell Again," *New York Times* (August 16, 1926), rep. In *New York Times Film Reviews*, Vol. 1, p. 926.

37. Hubert, *Hollywood*, p. 47.

38. Ernst Lubitsch, "The Motion Picture Is the Youngest of All the Muses," in *The Truth about the Movies by the Stars*, ed. Laurence A. Hughes (Hollywood: Hollywood Publishers, 1924), pp. 349, 351. One might wonder if a seemingly ephemeral article like this or other short pieces signed by Lubitsch during this period were in fact ghost-written. Most of them seem, however, quite specific in their discussions and focus on issues that we know to have been of interest to Lubitsch. They ring true as having actually been written by him (undoubtedly with some help with the English).

39. Mordaunt Hall, "A Calculating Villain," *New York Times* (October 6, 1924), rep. In *New York Times Film Reviews*, Vol. 1, p. 213.

40. Quoted in Eyman, *Ernst Lubitsch*, p. 184.

41. "The Student Prince," *Moving Picture World* 88, 4 (September 24, 1927): 250; Mordaunt Hall, "In Old Heidelberg," *New York Times* (September 11, 1927), rep. *New York Times Film Reviews*, Vol. 1, p. 388.

Notes to Chapter Six

1. Robert Florey, *Deux ans dans les studios américains* (Paris: Publications Jean-Pascal, 1926), p. 272.
2. Arnold Pressburger, "Aus der amerikanischen Filmindustrie," Pt. 1 *Lichtbildbühne* 14, 1 (January 1, 1920): 52.
3. Consul Frederich Simpish, "The Motion-Picture Business in Germany," *Commerce Reports* no. 89 (April 15, 1920): 305.
4. "Demetrius in Staaken," *Lichtbildbühne* 15, 28 (July 8, 1922): 16; "Grossfilmwerk Staaken," *Lichtbildbühne* 16, 23 (June 9, 1923): 14-15.
5. "25 Jahre Filmatalier," in *25 Jahre Kinematograph* (Berlin: Scherl, 1931), p. 66; "Was die 'L.B.B.' erzählt," *Lichtbildbühne* 16, 4 (January 27, 1922): 28; L'Estrange Fawcett, *Films, Facts and Forecasts* (London: G. Bles, 1927), p. 120.
6. "Jupiter-Kunstlicht," *Lichtbildbühne* 15, 29 (July 15, 1922): 35; Erich Pommer, "Hands across the Sea in Movie Development," *New York Times* (January 16, 1927): sec. 7, p. 5.
7. "Die Herstellung optische Gläser – Die Bell & Howell-Camera," *Lichtbildbühne* 14, 42 (October 15, 1921): 50-51; Karl J. Fritzsche, "Die Aussichten für den deutschen Filmexport," *Lichtbildbühne* Luxusnummer (1922/1923), n.p.
8. "Charles Rosher Goes to Berlin," *American Cinematographer* 6, 6 (September 1925): 24; "Mitchell Cameras, Equipment Go to Studios in Germany," *American Cinematographer* 5, 9 (December 1924): 9.
9. C. A. Luperti, "Ein Brief aus Amerika," *Die Kinotechnik* 3, 16 (November 1921): 607.
10. Otto Stindt, "Aufnahmelampen," *Die Filmtechnik* 4, 9 (April 28, 1928): 160-161.
11. Otto Stindt, "Lichttechnische Lügen," *Die Filmtechnik* 2, 19 (September 18, 1926): 375-377.
12. Otto Stindt, "Die Befreiung vom Hintergrund," *Die Filmtechnik* 3, 12 (June 11, 1927): 220-222.
13. For a discussion of the soft style in Hollywood cinematography, see David Bordwell, Janet Staiger, and Kristin Thompson, *The Classical Hollywood Cinema: Film Style and Mode of Production to 1960* (London: Routledge and Kegan Paul, 1985), pp. 287-293.
14. A. V. Barsy, "Soft Focus," *Die Filmtechnik* 2, 14 (July 10, 1926): 277-278.
15. Heinz Umbehr and Sophus Wangöe, "Versuch um den Soft-focus," *Die Filmtechnik* 4, 25 (December 10, 1928): 482-486; Rosher's lens is discussed and illustrated on page 485.
16. Walther Reimann, "Ein Nachwort zum 'Caligari'-Film," *Die Filmtechnik* 1, 10 (October 5, 1926): 221. The first part of this article was published under the same title in *Die Filmtechnik* 1, 9 (September 25, 1925: 192-193. For other contributions to the painter-vs.-architect debate, see Walther Reimann, "Filmarchtektur-Film-

architekt?" *Gebrauchsgraphik* no. 6 (1924/1925), rep. in Rolf Aurich and Wolfgang Jacosen, eds., *Werkstatt Film: Selbstverständnis und Visionene von Filmleuten der zwanziger Jahre* (Munich: edition text + kritik, 1998), pp. 111-115; Karl Freund took the painterly position in "Die Berufung des Kameramannes," *Die Filmtechnik* 2, 2 (January 20, 1926): 22-24; Reimann replied to both Freund and L. Witlin's (see next endnote) articles in "Filmarchitechtur – heute und morgen?" *Die Filmtechnik* 2, 4 (February 20, 1926): 64-65; and Lothar Holland, "Die Szenerie," *Die Filmtechnik* 3, 11 (May 28, 1927): 198-199. Erno Metzner may have helped initiate the debate by a passage in a 1924 article: "To envision and fashion a painterly film material, that I take to be the path for the culture of décor." See his "Die Kultur der Dekorations," in E. Beyfuss and A. Kossowsky, eds., *Das Kulturfilmbuch* (Berlin: Carl P. Chryse-lius'scher Verlag, 1934), rep. Aurich and Jacobsen, *Werkstatt Film*, pp. 104-106.

17. L. Witlin, "Filmarchitect oder Filmmaler?" *Die Filmtechnik* 2, 3 (February 5, 1926): 43-44. Witlin's article replied specifically to Reimann's "Filmarchitektur-Film-architekt?"

18. Georg Otto Stindt, "Bildschnitt," *Die Filmtechnik* 2, 7 (April 3, 1926): 129.

19. Walther Reimann, "Filmbauten und Raumkunst," *Das grosse Bilderbuch des Films* (Berlin: Film-Kurier, 1926), rep. in Aurich and Jacobsen, *Werkstatt Film*, pp. 115-119.

20. Stindt, "Bildschnitt," pp. 130-131.

21. Adolf Kobitzsch, "Kontinuität der Bilderfolge," *Die Filmtechnik* 3, 25 (December 10, 1927): 438-439.

22. "Die entfesselte Kamera," *Ufa-Magazin* 2, 13 (March 25-31, 1927): n.p.

23. Ewald Andre Dupont, "Camera Work on Scenes in 'Variety,'" *New York Times* (July 1926): Sec. 7, p. 2.

24. Mordaunt Hall, "Lubitsch Rings the Bell Again," *The New York Times Film Reviews 1913-1968* (New York: New York Times & Arno Press, 1970), vol. I, p. 926; Sime, "So This Is Paris," *Variety Film Reviews* (New York: Garland, 1983), vol. III, n.p. (August 18, 1928).

25. Florey, *Deux ans*, p. 121.

Notes to Epilogue

1. Peter Bogdanovich, "The Director I Never Met" in his *Who the Devil Made It* (New York: Alfred A. Knopf, 1997), p. 31.

2. Cameron Crowe, *Conversations with Wilder* (New York: Alfred A. Knopf, 1999), pp. 32-33.

3. Herman G. Weinberg, *The Lubitsch Tough: A Critical Study* (New York: E.P. Dutton & Co., 1968), p. 25.

4. Weinberg, *The Lubitsch Touch*, p. 287. The quotation comes from a letter from Fair-banks to Weinberg written in 1968.

5. Danny, "Pictures," *The Film Daily* 34, 71 (December 24, 1925): 1.

6. "The Screen," *New York Times* (April 18, 1921), rep. in *New York Times Film Reviews* (New York: New York Times and Arno Press), vol. I, p. 93.

7. Mordaunt Hall, "Music and Wine," *New York Times* (August 5, 1925), rep. in *New York Times Film Reviews*, vol. 1, p. 268.

8. Fred, "*Kiss Me Again*," *Variety* (August 5, 1925), rep. in *Variety Film Reviews*, vol II, n.p.

9. "So This Is Paris," *The Film Daily* (August 15, 1926): 7.

10. Charles S. Sewell, "*Three Women*," *Moving Picture World* 70, 4 (September 27, 1924): 334.

11. Mordaunt Hall, "Lubitsch Rings the Bell Again," *New York Times* (August 16, 1926), rep. in *New York Times Film Reviews*, vol. I, p. 926.

12. "Lady Windermere's Fan," *The Film Daily* (December 6, 1925): 4.

13. Fred, "*Lady Windermere's Fan*," *Variety* (January 13, 1926), rep. in *Variety Film Reviews*, vol. III, n.p.

14. Charles S. Sewell, "*Lady Windermere's Fan* – Warner Brothers," *Moving Picture World* 77, 6 (December 12, 1925): 575.

15. Mordaunt Hall, "In Old Heidelberg," *New York Times* (September 22, 1927), rep. in *New York Times Film Reviews*, vol. I, p. 388.

16. A. Van Buren Powell, "Straight from the Shoulder Reports," *Moving Picture World* 68, 3 (May 17, 1924): 299.

17. Ernst Lubitsch, "Film Directing," *The World Film Encyclopedia*, ed. Clarence Winchester (London: The Amalgamated Press, 1933), p. 442. In a 1947 *American Cinematographer* article, the author uses the phrase in the singular and quotes Lubitsch concerning it:

"The Lubitsch touch? It's best described by the author himself when he gave this answer to an inquiring reporter:

"What exactly, you ask me, is the Lubitsch touch? It's the king in his bedroom with his suspenders hanging; it's the gondola hauling garbage in Venice while the gondolier sings romantically; it's the husband bidding his wife a melancholy good-bye and then dashing madly for the nearest telephone booth. It's naughty and it's gay. It's based on the theory that at least twice a day the most dignified of human beings is ridiculous."

By that point, Lubitsch clearly had his answer down pat. Precisely when in the period between 1933 and 1947 Lubitsch touches became the Lubitsch touch I will leave for historians of the director's sound period to discover. (See Mollie Merrick, "25 Years of the 'Lubitsch Touch' in Hollywood," *American Cinematographer* [July, 1947]: 258.)

Filmography

Dates indicated for Lubitsch's films are those of the premieres; from Hans Helmut Prinzler and Enno Patalas, Lubitsch (Munich: C. J. Bucher, 1984). Dates for the non-Lubitsch films are usually the year of the film's premiere; followed by the director's name (* *indicates film is lost*).

Lubitsch (chronologically)

Berlin

* DER RODELCAVALIER   March 1, 1918
* DER FALL ROSENTOPF   September 20, 1918
DIE AUGEN DER MUMIE MÂ   October 3, 1918
ICH MÖCHTE KEIN MANN SEIN   October, 1918
* DAS MÄDEL VOM BALLET   December 6, 1918
CARMEN   December 20, 1918
MEYER AUS BERLIN   January 17, 1919
* MEINE FRAU, DIE FILMSCHAUSPIELERIN   January 24, 1919
DIE AUSTERNPRINZESSIN   June 20, 1919
* RAUSCH   August 1, 1919
MADAME DUBARRY   September 18, 1919
DIE PUPPE   December 4, 1919
KOHLHIESELS TÖCHTER   March 9, 1920
ROMEO UND JULIA IM SCHNEE   March 12, 1920
SUMURUN   September 1, 1920
ANNA BOLEYN   December 14, 1920
DIE BERGKATZE   April 12, 1921
DAS WEIB DES PHARAO   February 21, 1922
DIE FLAMME   September 11, 1923

Hollywood

ROSITA   September 3, 1923
THE MARRIAGE CIRCLE   February 3, 1924
THREE WOMEN   October 5, 1924 (The print viewed at George Eastman House was a gift of the Cinémathèque Française, with the text of the replaced English intertitles provided by Warner Bros.)

FORBIDDEN PARADISE   October 27, 1924 (The print viewed at George Eastman House was made from a Czech nitrate print, loaned by MOMA; no
information on the source of the replaced English-language intertitles is
available.)

* KISS ME AGAIN   August 1,1925

LADY WINDERMERE'S FAN   December 1,1925

SO THIS IS PARIS   July 31, 1926

THE STUDENT PRINCE IN OLD HEIDELBERG   September 21, 1927

* THE PATRIOT   August 17, 1928

ETERNAL LOVE   May 11, 1929 (released in silent and sound versions)

Other Films Cited (Alphabetically)

ANSTÄNDIGE FRAU, EINE   1925 Paul Stein

BRÜDER KARAMASSOFF, DIE   1920 Carl Froelich

CABINET DES DR. CALIGARI, DER   1920 Robert Wiene

EHE DER FÜRSTIN DEMIDOFF, DIE   1921 Friedrich Zelnick

EIFERSUCHT   1925 Karl Grune

HEIMKEHR   1928 Joe May

HURRAH! ICH LEBE!   1928 Wilhelm Thiele

I. N. R. I.: DIE KATASTROPHE EINES VOLKES   1920 Ludwig Beck

LANDSTRASSE UND GROSSSTADT   1921 Carl Wilhelm

LETZTE DROSCHKE VON BERLIN, DIE   1926 Carl Boese

LETZTE MANN, DER   1924 F. W. Murnau

LIEBSCHAFTEN DES HEKTOR DALMORE, DIE   1921 Richard Oswald

MANN IM FEUER, DER   1926 Erich Waschneck

MARIONETTEN DES TEUFELS   1920 Friedrich Feher and Johannes Brandt

METROPOLIS   1927 Fritz Lang

MR. WU   1918 Lupu Pick

NACHT DER EINBRECHER, DIE   1921 ?

NERVEN   1919 Robert Reinert

PANZERGEWÖLBE, DAS   1926 Lupu Pick

ROSE BERND   1919 Alfred Halm

STRASSE, DIE   1923 Karl Grune

SYLVESTER   1923 Lupu Pick

TROMMELN ASIENS, DIE   1921 Uwe Jens Krafft

VARIÉTÉ   1925 E. A. Dupont

VATER WERDEN IST NICHT SCHWER   1926 Erich Schönfelder

VOM TÄTER FEHLT JEDE SPUR   1928 Constantin J. David

WEISSE PFAU, DER   1920 E. A. Dupont

WUNDERBARE LÜGE DER NINA PETROWNA, DIE   1929 Hanns Schwarz

Films Viewed But Not Cited

I have not listed Expressionist films.

ABWEGE   1928 G. W. Pabst

ALTE GESETZ, DAS   1923 E. A. Dupont

AM RANDE DER WELT   1927 Karl Grune

ANDERS ALS DIE ANDEREN   1919 Richard Oswald

BLAUE MAUS, DIE   1928 Johannes Guter

BRÜDER SCHELLENBERG, DIE   1926 Karl Grune

BÜCHSE DER PANDORA, DIE   1928 G. W. Pabst

CARMEN VON ST. PAULI, DIE   1928 Erich Waschneck

DAME MIT DEM TIGERFELL, DIE   1927 Willi Wolff

DAME MIT DER MASKE, DIE   1928 Wilhelm Thiele

DIRNENTRAGODIE   1927 Bruno Rahn

DR. MONNIER UND DIE FRAUEN   1928 Gustav Molander

DÜRFEN WIR SCHWEIGEN?   1926 Richard Oswald

FARMER AUS TEXAS, DER   1925 Joe May

FINANZEN DES GROSSHERZOGS, DIE   1923 F. W. Murnau

FRIDERICUS REX: EIN KÖNIGSSCHIKSAL, Pt. 4   1923 Arzen von Cserépy

GANG IN DER NACHT, DER   1920 F. W. Murnau

GEHEIME MACHT, DIE   1927 Erich Waschneck

GEHEIMNISSE EINER SEELE   1926 G. W. Pabst

GEIGER VON FLORENZ, DER   1926 Paul Czinner

GESCHLECHT IN FESSELN   1928 Wilhelm Dieterle

GIRL VON DER REVUE, DAS   1928 Richard Eichberg

HAMLET   1920 Svend Gade

HAUS AM MEER, DAS   1924 Fritz Kaufmann

HERRIN DER WELT, DIE   1920 Joe May

INDISCHE GRABMAL, DAS   1921 Joe May

KAMPF UM DIE SCHOLLE   1924 Erich Waschneck

KAMPF UMS MATTERNHORN, DER   1928 Mario Bonnard and Nunzio
    Malasomma

KÄMPFENDE HERZEN   1921 Fritz Lang

LEIBEIGENEN, DIE   1927 Richard Eichberg

LIEBE DER JEANNE NEY, DIE   1927 G. W. Pabst

MANON LESCAUT   1926 Arthur Robison

OPIUM   1919 Robert Reinert

OTHELLO   1922 Dimitri Buchowetski

PEST IN FLORENZ, DIE   1919 Otto Rippert

PHANTOM   1922 F. W. Murnau

REIGEN, DER   1920 Richard Oswald

Seine Frau, die Unbekannte   1923 Benjamin Christensen
Spinnen, Die   1919-1920 Fritz Lang
Spione   1928 Fritz Lang
Student von Prague, Der   1926 Henrik Galeen
Tatjana   1923 Robert Dinesen
Unheimliche Geschichten   1919 Richard Oswald
Vanina   1922 Arthur von Gerlach
verlorene Schatten, Der   1921 Rochus Gliese and Paul Wegener
wandernde Bild, Das   1920 Fritz Lang
Weber, Die   1927 Friedrich Zelnick

Index

Film Culture in Transition
General Editor: *Thomas Elsaesser*

Double Trouble: Chiem van Houweninge on Writing and Filming
Thomas Elsaesser, Robert Kievit and Jan Simons (eds.)

Writing for the Medium: Television in Transition
Thomas Elsaesser, Jan Simons and Lucette Bronk (eds.)

Between Stage and Screen: Ingmar Bergman Directs
Egil Törnqvist

The Film Spectator: From Sign to Mind
Warren Buckland (ed.)

Film and the First World War
Karel Dibbets and Bert Hogenkamp (eds.)

A Second Life: German Cinema's First Decades
Thomas Elsaesser (ed.)

Fassbinder's Germany: History Identity Subject
Thomas Elsaesser

Cinema Futures: Cain, Abel or Cable? The Screen Arts in the Digital Age
Thomas Elsaesser and Kay Hoffmann (eds.)

Audiovisions: Cinema and Television as Entr'Actes in History
Siegfried Zielinski

Joris Ivens and the Documentary Context
Kees Bakker (ed.)

Ibsen, Strindberg and the Intimate Theatre: Studies in TV Presentation
Egil Törnqvist

The Cinema Alone: Essays on the Work of Jean-Luc Godard 1985-2000
Michael Temple and James S. Williams (eds.)

Micropolitics of Media Culture: Reading the Rhizomes of Deleuze and
Guattari
Patricia Pisters and Catherine M. Lord (eds.)

Malaysian Cinema, Asian Film: Border Crossings and National Cultures
William van der Heide

Film Culture in Transition
General Editor: *Thomas Elsaesser*

Double Trouble: Chiem van Houweninge on Writing and Filming
Thomas Elsaesser, Robert Kievit and Jan Simons (eds.)

Writing for the Medium: Television in Transition
Thomas Elsaesser, Jan Simons and Lucette Bronk (eds.)

Between Stage and Screen: Ingmar Bergman Directs
Egil Törnqvist

The Film Spectator: From Sign to Mind
Warren Buckland (ed.)

Film and the First World War
Karel Dibbets and Bert Hogenkamp (eds.)

A Second Life: German Cinema's First Decades
Thomas Elsaesser (ed.)

Fassbinder's Germany: History Identity Subject
Thomas Elsaesser

Cinema Futures: Cain, Abel or Cable? The Screen Arts in the Digital Age
Thomas Elsaesser and Kay Hoffmann (eds.)

Audiovisions: Cinema and Television as Entr'Actes in History
Siegfried Zielinski

Joris Ivens and the Documentary Context
Kees Bakker (ed.)

Ibsen, Strindberg and the Intimate Theatre: Studies in TV Presentation
Egil Törnqvist

The Cinema Alone: Essays on the Work of Jean-Luc Godard 1985-2000
Michael Temple and James S. Williams (eds.)

Micropolitics of Media Culture: Reading the Rhizomes of Deleuze and Guattari
Patricia Pisters and Catherine M. Lord (eds.)

Malaysian Cinema, Asian Film: Border Crossings and National Cultures
William van der Heide

Film Front Weimar: Representations of the First World War in German Films of the Weimar Period (1919-1933)
Bernadette Kester

Camera Obscura, Camera Lucida: Essays in Honor of Annette Michelson
Richard Allen and Malcolm Turvey (eds.)

Jean Desmet and the Early Dutch Film Trade
Ivo Blom

City of Darkness, City of Light: Émigré Filmmakers in Paris 1929-1939
Alastair Phillips

The Last Great American Picture Show: New Hollywood Cinema in the 1970s
Thomas Elsaesser, Alexander Horwath and Noel King (eds.)

Harun Farocki: Working on the Sight-Lines
Thomas Elsaesser (ed.)